The

Guide to

The

Kid's

Guide to

Research

BY DEBORAH HEILIGMAN

WITH THE COOPERATION OF THE NEW YORK PUBLIC LIBRARY

SCHOLASTIC
REFERENCE

For Nancy Laties Feresten

Copyright © 1998 by Scholastic Inc. and The New York Public Library, Astor, Lenox, and Tilden Foundations.
Illustrations © 1998 by David Cain.

All rights reserved. Published by Scholastic Inc.
SCHOLASTIC and associated logos are trademarks and/or registered trademarks of Scholastic Inc.
The name "The New York Public Library" is a registered trademark and the property of The New York Public Library, Astor, Lenox, and Tilden Foundations.

No part of this publication may be reproduced, or stored in a retrieval system, or transmitted in any form or by any means, electronic, mechanical, photocopying, recording, or otherwise, without written permission of the publisher. For information regarding permission, write to Scholastic Inc., Attention: Permissions Department, 555 Broadway, New York, NY 10012.

Heiligman, Deborah.
The kid's guide to research / by Deborah Heiligman.
p.   cm.
Includes index.
Summary: Provides guidance on how to do research, including how to use libraries and their resources, the Internet, and other sources such as interviews and surveys.
ISBN 0-590-30715-0 (hc)—ISBN 0-590-30716-9 (pb)
1. Libraries—Juvenile literature.   2. Information retrieval—Juvenile literature.
3. Report writing—Juvenile literature. [1. Research.   2. Libraries.]   I. Title.
Z710.H38   1998   97-28939
025.5′24—dc21   CIP   AC

10 9 8 7 6 5   01 02
Printed in the U.S.A. 23
First printing, August 1999

Design by David Saylor

Previously published as *The New York Public Library Kid's Guide to Research*

CONTENTS

INTRODUCTION

When I was learning to do research, a librarian gave me great advice. She said, "When you start any research project, ask yourself, 'What do I know, and what do I need to know?' "

When you do research, ask yourself these questions over and over again. The answers will guide you through your research and make your job much easier.

When you first ask yourself, "What do I know?" the answer is likely to be, "Not much." The answer to the second question, "What do I need to know?" is going to be "Everything."

The idea of researching "everything" is scary. How do you do it? *One step at a time.*

Don't be scared. You've been doing research all your life. When you want to find out what time a TV show is on, you do research. When you need to call someone and you don't know his or her phone number, you do research. When you want something to eat and you open up the refrigerator, you do research.

If you're at all nosy or curious, you are a natural-born

researcher. Do you wonder what's in a letter your mom got? Do you want to listen to a conversation your sister is having? Would you like to know what your favorite teacher does on weekends? All research takes is some natural curiosity and a little know-how. You've already got the curiosity. This book will help you learn good researching techniques and skills.

When you research a topic, you go from clue to clue, from fact to fact, building up information until you know your subject really well. You  find information in books, magazine articles, and on the Internet. You get answers from people, from places, and even from TV shows. When you've done a lot of research and gotten information from many sources, then you put it all together in your own way. That's research!

You can learn the logical steps of doing research by reading this book from the beginning to the end. But you don't have to. You can get help by looking up subjects in the index or the table of contents.

When you start a research project, give yourself plenty of time. Don't put off your research until the last minute. You want the time to explore, follow cool leads, go where your subject takes you. If you start early, you will have time to send away for information, interview people, explore the Internet, maybe even take a trip. Doing research can be an exciting adventure. Go for it!

Choosing a Topic

Have you been assigned a specific topic to research? If so, you can skip this chapter.

Did your teacher give you a general topic, such as AN ANIMAL or A PRESIDENT OF THE UNITED STATES or SOMETHING IN OUR STATE'S HISTORY, for you to narrow down? Or are you allowed to choose your own topic, in any subject, about anything? Choosing your own topic—or narrowing a general topic—can be a lot of fun, but sometimes it's hard to get started. *Any* animal? *Anything* in the history of our state? *Anything* at all? How do you go about choosing a topic that will work for a report?

1. Do some thinking, reading, browsing, and hunting. (If a subject just jumps out at you, or you've always wanted to find out about a certain topic, skip this part and go straight to number 2.)

Before you choose your subject, look around. If you're looking for a new pair of sneakers, do you just walk into the store, pick up the first pair you see, and buy it? No, you look around, pick up some shoes, look at them, and when you find some you like, you try them on.

It's the same thing when you're choosing a subject. Go to the library. Page through an encyclopedia. Browse through the shelves or ask a librarian to point you to the section on technology, or art, or whatever general subject you'd like to explore. Pull down some books and browse through them. If a topic interests you, write it down, and do some more reading about it.

2. Ask for suggestions.
Ask other people for suggestions. Your older brother might remember a cool report somone in his class did on Benedict Arnold. Your aunt might tell you about amazing fish she saw the last time

she went snorkling. You could also post the question on-line—on a kids' message board, in a kids' chatroom, or in a newsgroup. "I'm looking for a good science topic to do a report on. I'm in fifth grade. Any ideas?" Or, more specific: "I'd like to do a report on one aspect of the Civil War. I'm in seventh grade. Does anybody have any ideas?"

3. Try it on for size. Now that you've chosen a topic, you have to make sure it fits. There are two requirements for a good fit: One, it has to interest you. Two, you have to be able to find enough information about it. To find out if a topic is interesting to you, start reading! Look in the dictionary and the encyclopedia first. If you start to yawn or wonder if you can go see a movie this weekend, then it's not the topic for you. Remember, you're going to have to live with this subject for quite a while. You'd better love it.

To figure out if there's enough information available on your topic, check the encyclopedia, the book catalog, and a magazine index. If you can't find information about your topic in those three places, it may be difficult to research. Ask a librarian for help. She might help you modify your topic so that you will be able to find information. Or you may have to find another topic to try on.

4. Think about your assignment. Will your topic meet the requirements for the assignment? Your topic not only has to fit you, it has to fit the assignment. If your teacher said you'd have to do an interview, make sure you know of a person you could interview about the topic. If you have to include graphs and charts, does your subject lend itself to graphs and charts? If your report has to be a certain length, judge as best you can if you will be able to write enough about the topic to fill that requirement.

5. Sleep on it. Give yourself a day or two to think about your topic. If you're still excited about the subject in a few days, then go for it. And have fun doing the research!

2

Going to the Library

Go to the library as soon as possible after you have your assignment or as soon as your teacher has approved the topic you have chosen.

Research always takes longer than you think it will. So you should give yourself plenty of time. The more time you have, the sooner you'll understand the basics of your topic, and the more time you'll have to do other kinds of research, such as surfing the Internet, interviewing people, digging in attics, and visiting museums. Also, the sooner you get to the library, the better a *selection of materials you'll have.* A lot of other kids are going to be doing reports at the same time you are. You don't want them to take out the books you need, do you?

BE PREPARED

To make the most out of your trip—or trips—to the library, always be prepared. You should:

Understand your assignment. If you have any questions about what you're supposed to do, ask your teacher before you go to the library.

Bring your assignment. If your teacher handed out an assignment sheet, bring that to the library. You might need to refer to it, and the librarian will want to see it when you ask for help. If you wrote down in your own words what your teacher said, bring that.

Bring your library card with you. If you don't have one yet, bring some identification with your address on it so you can get one.

Bring change to make photocopies. Some of the information you find may be in encyclopedias, dictionaries, other reference books, and current issues of magazines. You will not be able to check these sources out of the library, and you may not have time to take notes on everything. You'll want to make photocopies of the pages you need. Then, at home, you'll read those pages and take notes.

Bring a notebook or note cards to take notes and record the sources you use.

Bring at least two pens or pencils.

Bring along any other supplies you think you might need. You might want an extra eraser, a calculator, a ruler, your textbook, rubber bands for your note cards, an extra notebook, bookmarks, or sticky notes.

Bring a good-sized backpack or tote bag. You'll need it to carry your supplies to the library and to carry home all the materials you're going to check out.

Allow plenty of time in the library. You're not going to just run in, find what you need, and run out. Leave yourself time in case you hit some dead ends, or in case you find a lot of good stuff and you want to keep on going. For your first trip to the library, plan to be there for at least one or two hours.

Know what time the library closes. If you're being dropped off, tell your ride what time to come pick you up. Make it fifteen minutes before the library closes. Most libraries have you check out your books by then.

ASK YOUR LIBRARIAN FOR HELP

When you're doing your research, you will hit roadblocks, dead ends, questions, and problems. Where do you go for help? The best person to ask is a librarian. Reference and children's librarians want you to ask for help. Here's when and how to do it:

If you're having trouble finding information, or even a specific book, don't just nose around and decide that the library doesn't have what you're looking for. Go to the reference desk, or to the children's or young adult librarian, and ask for help. The perfect book might just be sitting in the back room on a cart, waiting to be shelved. "The child who asks gets the jewels," says one librarian.

If you can't find what you're looking for in the card or computer catalog, maybe that's because the information is not to be found in a book. Or maybe you're not looking it up in the best way. A librarian can help you search in a different, perhaps better, way. A librarian can also help you find information in other places, such as magazines, journals, the vertical file, tapes, the Internet, or even in books that might not have shown up in the catalog.

Not only can librarians help you search, they can also tell you if the search isn't going to turn up anything. Sometimes you get an impossible assignment or have given yourself one. The librarian can then either help you change the focus of your report or write a note to your teacher telling why this assignment won't work.

Ask the librarian to show you *how* to find things in the library. That is more valuable than having the librarian (or your parent) just pick out a book for you. You will be able to use the research techniques you learn forever—if you do the research yourself. So don't say to the librarian, "I need a book on Benedict Arnold." Say, "Could you please show me how to find information on Benedict Arnold?" Keep in mind that the librarian is there to help you do your work, not to do the work for you.

Be patient and wait your turn. The librarian may be trying to help three other people with three totally different subjects all at the same time, while trying to remember where the stuff on your subject is.

Thank the librarian for the help.

If a librarian really helps, let him or her know. Bring in your finished report. The librarian would love to see it.

3

Reference Books

Your first stop in the library should be the reference section. That's the section that has encyclopedias and dictionaries of all kinds, almanacs, atlases, and reference books you've never even heard of.

Most reference books are noncirculating, which means you cannot check them out. So you will have to use these books in the library, unless you are fortunate enough to have some reference books at home.

Some libraries have older encyclopedias that are in circulation; you can take home the volume or two that you need, just the way you check out a book.

THE DICTIONARY

Use the dictionary to get acquainted with your topic. You can look up your topic in a regular dictionary, a kids' dictionary, or a dictionary on a computer.

You will get some quick, basic facts from the dictionary, including the definition and the origin of the word. If you're lucky, there will also be a picture. In the definition you might find some other *key words* about your topic. The dictionary will also tell you how to pronounce your topic, which will save you from embarrassment when you're asking for help or doing an oral report. (If it's a difficult word to pronounce, write down the pronunciation so you don't forget it.) Suppose your topic is the marmoset. You know the marmoset is a type of monkey, but that's all you know. So you look it up in the dictionary. If you look in one dictionary, here's what you'll find:

mar•mo•set n. (mär´ mə-sĕt´, -zĕt´) Any of various small monkeys of the genera Callithrix, Cebuella, Saguinus, and Leontideus, found in tropical forests of the Americas. They have soft, dense fur, tufted ears, and long tails. [Middle English, from Old French marmoset, grotesque figure.]

Cool! You love monkeys. And the word *marmoset* is from the Old French for "grotesque figure." To top it off, in the margin there is a picture of a golden or lion-headed marmoset that you just want to take home.

Aside from telling you that the marmoset is cool, the definition also gives you some information that you can use in your research.

🐾 There are different kinds of marmosets, which will make your report interesting.

🐾 They live in tropical forests. You may want to do some research on tropical forests to see what the marmoset's habitat is like.

🐾 You have some other ways you can look up your topic: *long-tailed monkeys, golden marmoset,* and *lion-headed marmoset.*

THE ENCYCLOPEDIA

After looking up your topic in the dictionary, your next stop should be an encyclopedia. An encyclopedia is a collection of articles on many topics. There are two kinds of encyclopedias—general (such as *The World Book, Compton's,* and *Encarta*) and special (such as *The Encyclopedia of the U.S. Presidency* and *Encyclopedia of the Dog*).

If your teacher says to you, "Don't use the encyclopedia," chances are that doesn't mean don't use one at all. It means don't use *only* an encyclopedia. (Double-check with the teacher to be sure.) An encyclopedia has a lot of useful information. It's not going to tell you everything you need to know, but it will tell you the basics and guide you to your next research steps. Like a dictionary entry, an encyclopedia article will also give you key words to use in your search.

A WORD ABOUT KEY WORDS

A very important part of researching is figuring out how to look up your topic. Sometimes it's really obvious. If you're doing a report on Arizona, the easiest way to find information on your topic is to look up *Arizona*. But sometimes there's more than one way to look up a topic.

Make a list of synonyms and related words for your topic. For example, if you're doing a report on cowboys who helped settle the West and Pacific Northwest, of course you should look up *cowboys*. But you could also look up these key words: *Oregon Trail; Dodge City; Chisholm Trail; Prairies; Indian Territory; Jesse James; Calamity Jane*. Many of these key words you will know only after you've done some research. That's why it's good to start your research with a dictionary and an encyclopedia.

Which key word to use depends on where you're looking. If you've found a book about monkeys, then you should look in the index under *marmoset*. But to find a book that has marmosets in it, search the library's card or computer catalog under *monkey*. On the Internet, where narrow searches are better, you should search under *marmoset* or even *lion-headed marmoset*.

General Encyclopedias

A general encyclopedia is made up of many volumes, or books. The volumes are set up in alphabetical or numerical order. Usually there is one volume per letter of the alphabet. Some letters have more entries and need two volumes; some letters have fewer entries and share a volume. Encyclopedias also come on CD-ROMs that you use in a computer.

The articles in an encyclopedia are usually written by experts in their fields. So you can feel reasonably certain that the information is correct.

It's a good idea to use the most up-to-date encyclopedia you can find. If you're doing a report on computer technology, you don't want an encyclopedia that is more than a year old, because computer technology changes practically every day. To find out how old the encyclopedia is, check the copyright date. (It is a good idea to check the copyright date on any book you use.) The copyright date is the date the book was published. You can find it on the copyright page, which is usually on the back of the title page. The copyright date has a © before it.

Keep in mind that a book or encyclopedia is written over the course of a year or a few years, and then it takes a certain amount of time (usually about a year) for the book to come out. So even an encyclopedia with this year's date on it will have information that is at least a year old.

The Index

Most people use an encyclopedia from the outside, looking up their topic in the volume with that letter on it. That often works, especially with a big subject such as Abraham Lincoln. For Abraham Lincoln you'd go to the **L** volume, where you'd find him listed alphabetically by his last name. Of course you'd find a huge article about our sixteenth president.

However, the best way to use an encyclopedia is to start at the back, with the index.

In a print encyclopedia, the index is in the last one or two volumes of the whole set. The index lists, in alphabetical order, every topic that is in the encyclopedia, with the page numbers where you can find the topic.

Starting with the index is a good idea for two reasons.

First, the index will tell you every place in the encyclopedia your topic is mentioned. This way you will get more information than if you had just looked under the main article.

Second, not all topics have their own articles. The index tells you where to look for those topics. For example, if you were researching minor league baseball and went to the **M** volume, you wouldn't find an article. But if you looked up *minor leagues* in the index, you'd find a section about this topic in the article on baseball. So instead of the **M** volume, you'd find information about minor league baseball in the **B** volume.

Looking Up a Topic

Suppose you're doing a report on the *Titanic*. You go to the index of *The World Book Encyclopedia*. You look up

Titanic. You'll find this listing: ***Titanic*** [ship] **T: 299** *with picture*. That tells you that the article is in volume **T**, on page 299, and that there is a picture with the article. Now, if you had just gone to the **T** volume and looked up *Titanic*, you would have found the main article, too. But the index also has these articles listed:

Exploration (Deep-sea exploration) **E:451–452**
Iceberg (Ice Patrols) **I:18**
Sarnoff, David **S:127**
Shipwreck (table: Major shipwrecks) **S:428**

By starting with the index, you already know four places in the encyclopedia to look for information about the *Titanic*. And right away you know there's a table you could include in your report if you need or want to. Also, the index gives you other interesting avenues to explore. What are ice patrols, and who was David Sarnoff? What does deep-sea exploration have to do with the *Titanic*?

For a CD-ROM encyclopedia, you use the search function to find what you're looking for. You can search the article topics or search in the index. Try both, but you'll get more "hits" (and find more information) by searching the index.

Reading an Encyclopedia Article

Usually you should read the entire encyclopedia article. Make sure to read all the parts of the article, not just the main text. A longer article in an encyclopedia will have sidebars (in the article on Lincoln in *The World Book Encyclopedia*, for example, are sidebars on important dates in his life, a box of quotations, and a look at the world at the time of President Lincoln).

If there are pictures in the article, look at them carefully. Pictures are a kind of visual research that add to your report. Wouldn't it be great to show or tell what Lincoln looked like as a boy?

Read the picture captions, too. They clarify information that is in the main part of the article and sometimes give new information.

Some articles have diagrams that help explain the topic. Some have graphs, charts, or tables. All of these things are filled with goodies—remember, as a researcher, you want to dig to uncover interesting facts, facts that somebody else might miss.

To help you navigate through the article, there are headings in boldface (dark) type. These **headings** announce what the section is about. Each section is also divided into subsections with **subheads**. For example, in the article on Lincoln, there is a section called **Early**

life. In that section, there are subheads: **Family background**, **Boyhood**, **Education**.

Heads and subheads are particularly helpful if you're researching just a part of a topic. If you're doing a report on one part of Lincoln's life, or you just need to find out a particular piece of information, you might want to skim the article. Read the heads and subheads first to find sections that have the information you need. Suppose you want to know what Lincoln said at his first inauguration. Skim through the article until you come to the section called **Lincoln's administration**. Under that heading you will find a section called **First inaugu-**

ration. In that section you'll find out what the theme of his speech was.

For Further Information

When you're finished reading the article, keep going. At the end of the article you will find a lot more information to help take you to your next step. There is a list of cross references, other articles in the encyclopedia that mention your subject. There is also a list of other books you might want to look at. Make a note of those articles and books. For example, at the end of the Lincoln article is the listing for a book of Lincoln's speeches. You could probably find the whole text of his inaugural address in that book. *When you're doing research, way leads to way.* One piece of information will lead you to another—just like clues on a treasure hunt.

Special Encyclopedias

Special encyclopedias are devoted to single subjects. There are encyclopedias about wildlife and encyclopedias about dogs. There's an encyclopedia of sports rules. There are encyclopedias about U.S. presidents, insects, science, endangered animals, technology, fashion, multicultural America, African Americans, the environment— you get the idea. These encyclopedias are especially helpful if you need to narrow your search for a topic. Suppose you are asked to do a report on a mammal— any mammal. Go to an encyclopedia that is devoted to mammals. Browse around, look at pictures, compare different animals, and see which one "speaks" to you.

Special encyclopedias can also be good if you need to compare things or find out a very specific fact. Suppose you need to find out which weighs more, on average: a golden retriever or a yellow Labrador. If you look in a dog encyclopedia, you will probably find the answer quickly and efficiently.

Since encyclopedias are usually noncirculating, they are always there in the reference department when you need them. If everybody in your class is doing a report on insects, you might find no books left. But the insect encyclopedia has to stay in the library.

Special encyclopedias are usually quite detailed and may tell you just as much as a book would in a shorter space. So sometimes a special encyclopedia can do the job of a book in your research.

OTHER REFERENCE BOOKS

In the reference section of your library, you will find many other terrific books. Like encyclopedias, most of these books must stay in the library; you can't check them out and take them home.

Almanacs and books of facts. Almanacs have basic information, lists, statistics, facts, and figures. Books of facts are just that—books full of facts. There are a number of different almanacs and books of facts. Some are updated each year. Some are just for kids.

Atlases. An atlas is a book of maps. There are world atlases and U.S. atlases; atlases with political maps, which show country, state, county, and town borders; atlases with topographical maps, which show land forms; and atlases with both. There are also historical and cultural atlases.

Field guides. Field guides are books that help you observe a specific topic, usually in nature and the outdoors. There are field guides to flowers, butterflies, rocks and minerals, trees, even weeds. Field guides are full of pictures, descriptions, and facts.

Biographical dictionaries. Biographical dictionaries have short profiles of famous people. Some biographical dictionaries are themed: scientists, writers, rock stars. These books are often in a multivolume set.

Telephone books. Many libraries have telephone books from across the country. You can look up the address and telephone number of a person, company, or organization in your town or anywhere else. There are also books to help kids find addresses of famous people.

Quotation books. A quotation book is a collection of sayings, quotations, lines from poems and songs, excerpts from speeches, etc. Look in the index under a subject, or look up an author or famous person to see what he or she is quoted as saying.

Thesauruses. A thesaurus is a book of synonyms. It is very helpful for finding key words.

Dictionaries. We've already talked about regular dictionaries, which are a great help when you're doing research. But there are also specialized dictionaries, such as dictionaries of sign language or dictionaries of fables.

Books about good books for kids. There are many collections of recommended books, and some of them list both fiction and nonfiction by subject. If you are having trouble finding books for kids about your topic, try looking in one of these books.

HOW TO TAKE NOTES

As you do your research, you'll find lots of information that you might want to use in your report. You can't keep it all in your head, so you have to take notes. Your teacher may tell you a specific way to take notes. If so, follow that method. If you don't have guidelines, here is one system for taking notes:

Get something to write on. A stack of 3″ x 5″ index cards or a spiral notebook works well. Some researchers like to use note cards because you can rearrange them once you start to write. Other people prefer to use a notebook to keep everything together in one place. (You can also use a combination of the two: note cards that are bound together and perforated so you can rip them out later.)

Keep a list of your sources. Each time you use a new source—book, magazine or newspaper article, Web site, map, pamphlet—add it to your list of sources or make a special source card for it. Your source card (or list) should have all the information you'll need for your bibliography. Write down the first and last name of the author, the title, publisher and copyright date. For an article you'll need the pages, too. Make sure to write down dates and people you talk to if you do an interview, make a research trip, or perform an experiment.

Write down anything that you think you can use in your report. You can write each new fact or piece of information on a separate information card or page, if you want. Put a heading at the top of the card or page, such as **BEES—making honey** or **BEES—role of drones.**

Don't copy the information exactly, word for word, unless you are going to quote someone. If you do write it down exactly, put it in quotation marks. If you use the words exactly as they are written in a book and don't put that section in quotation marks, you're copying someone else's work. That is called plagiarism, and it's against the law. Besides, remember that research is not just copying what other people say. You get information from many sources and then put it together in your own way.

Note the source. After you've written down a
piece of information, write down which source it
came from. Because you have the whole source
on your list or source card, you can write down
just the author's name or part of the title on
each note. Write down what page it is on, too,
so you can check it later
if you need to. Some
researchers like to
give each source a
letter or a number.
For example, for a pro-
ject on lions, the first book

you use might be *Big Cats* by Seymour Simon.
You could call that source **1** and just write a **1** on
the card or paper every time you write down
notes from that book. Or, if you want to get
fancy, you can have a different-colored index card
for each source.

Don't forget: If you photocopy something in the
library, make sure to write down where it came
from so you won't get home and think, "Oh, no, I
don't have the source for this."

Make some quick notes. If you come across

some information and you're not sure you're going to need it, you can make just a short note of
it. But make sure you write down where you saw
it so you can go back to it later. For example, "In
NYPL Kid's Guide to Research, p. 25, info about
taking notes. Go back to?"

4

Books on Specific Topics

You've gotten a lot of basic facts by researching in reference books. Ask yourself those questions again now: "What do I know?" "What do I need to know?" Write down some specific questions you still need answers to. Write down the general areas in which you need to learn more. It's time to move on to books on specific topics.

This chapter will show you how to find books on your subject. Sometimes it will be easy—right there on the shelf will be three books that tell you what you need to know. But sometimes it will be trickier to find books that you can use.

If your topic is very narrow, it may not have a book of its own. You'll have to look in books about a larger, more general topic. For example, if you're doing research on rainbows, you might have to look in books about weather or colors or light.

On the other hand, if your subject is large, you may find many books—even too many books—about it. Your library may have more than one hundred books about the Civil War, for example. In that case, you will need to find the books that can best tell you what you want to know.

Your job is to find the best books you can for your research. Start with books that are written for children. They may have everything you need. But if you're an advanced reader, or you want to delve further into the subject, or you are having trouble finding books on your subject in the children's section, you may want to look at young adult and adult sections as well.

THE CATALOG

In your library there is a listing of *all* the books in the library. This listing is called a catalog. Some library catalogs also include books that can be found in other libraries in the library system. These books are not in your library, but you can order them. Many libraries have their books indexed on computerized catalogs. But some, including many school libraries, still use the "old-fashioned" card catalog. Ask your librarian to show you how to use your library's catalog the first time you use it.

In a catalog, each book is listed by its author, title, and subject.

If you know you want a specific book (perhaps it was

listed at the end of an encyclopedia article, or a friend told you about it, or the librarian recommended it), then you can look it up by the author or the title. Just look in alphabetical order in the card file or search on the computer. That's pretty easy.

But what if you don't have a specific book in mind?

What if you just have a topic? Then you look it up by subject.

HOW TO SEARCH BY SUBJECT

When you're searching by subject, the trick is to look up a subject that is narrow but not too narrow. Let's say you're doing a report on the frilled lizard. Would you search under *frilled lizard*? You could try, but chances are you won't find a book that way. *Frilled lizard* is too specific. Would you search under *reptiles*? You could, but then you'd get books on crocodiles and turtles and dinosaurs. *Reptiles* is too general. The best word to search under is *lizard*. If you don't come up with any books, or enough books, then go ahead and search under a broader topic, in this case *reptiles*.

Look at the titles of the books for ones that would be most likely to have information about the frilled lizard. (A book called *Small Reptiles* is more likely to have a section about lizards in it than a book called *All About Dinosaurs*.) But not all titles tell exactly what's in the book. You may have to go to the shelf and pull down some books to judge their usefulness.

The following guidelines will help you use any catalog efficiently.

Make sure you are spelling the words correctly. If you're looking for books on football, you're not going to find them if you type in *footsball* or *fotball*.

Use limiters when doing your search. Suppose you're researching football in the 1990s. With most computerized catalogs you can limit your search to a time period. If you can't figure out how to do it yourself, ask a librarian for help. You might also want to limit your search to children's books. So you might type in *football juvenile literature*.

Use Boolean operators. Boolean operators are words that help you limit or expand your search. The Boolean operators are AND, OR, NOT, and sometimes EXCEPT. Some systems use pluses and minuses instead of AND or NOT. (Ask your librarian to explain your system.)

Boolean operators are named for George Boole (1815–1864), who was an English mathematician and one of the founding fathers of mathematical logic. His work inspired a branch of mathematics called Boolean algebra. It deals with the relationships between sets, which makes sense for searches, because you are look-ing for connections between words and topics.

Using the correct Boolean operators can save you a lot of time and aggravation. Suppose you are doing a re-port on nuclear power. If you type in *nuclear*, you will get books about nuclear power and nuclear war and nu-clear weapons and nuclear families. But if you type in *nuclear* AND *power* or even *nuclear* AND *power* NOT *weapons*, you will get a list of books on your topic.

Try synonyms for different key words. If you're having trouble finding your subject, perhaps a synonym would work better. Look back at the notes you took while reading the dictionary and the encyclopedia. Are

 there any synonyms there you could try? You can also look up your topic in a thesaurus and try the synonyms you find there. Suppose you are doing a report on germs, but nothing comes up when you type in *germ* (except books about Germany). Try typing in *bacte-ria*, *virus*, or *microbe*. Sometimes near synonyms or closely related subjects will work, too. This is especially helpful if the word you're using is slang, or new. Perhaps

you're doing a report on cyberspace. But when you type in *cyberspace*, nothing comes up. Try typing in *Internet* or *World Wide Web*.

Write down the call numbers of the books. The call number is the combination of numbers and letters in the corner of the card or computer screen. It might look like this:

597.31

SCH

Also write down the title and author of each book. This will make it a lot easier to find the book on the shelf. (In some libraries you can print out a list of the books you want to look for. That will save you the time of writing everything down. Ask the librarian about it.)

Call Numbers

After you've looked up your subject in the card or computer catalog, you should have a list of books with their call numbers. Now you just have to *find* the books. That's what the call numbers are for. A call number is a kind of address that tells you where a book "lives," or is shelved. At the end of each row of shelves is a sign that tells you which call numbers can be found on that row.

Most libraries use the Dewey decimal system to organize and shelve their books. This system was developed by a librarian named Melvil Dewey. Before he came up with the system in 1876, books were put on shelves the way each librarian chose. You had to depend on the librarian's help to find the books you wanted. That wasn't so bad when there weren't that many books. But now, with millions of books in the world and huge libraries, we are lucky that Melvil Dewey made up his system.

The Dewey decimal system assigns each topic a number, so all the books on that topic wind up on the same shelf or group of shelves. Because most libraries are organized by the Dewey decimal system, you can go into just about any library and find all the books on a certain topic together.

Once you have found out the call number or numbers for the subject you're researching, you can go to the shelves and browse the books with those call numbers. Sometimes this is more efficient than doing your hunting on the catalog. (Some libraries, mostly large college libraries, use a different system, developed by the Library of Congress. If you are working in a library that uses the Library of Congress system, ask the librarian to get you started finding your call numbers.)

In some libraries, the call numbers are the same whether the book is in the adult, young adult, or children's section. But sometimes the call numbers in the children's section are shortened or begin with J, for

Juvenile. If you're having trouble finding a particular book in the children's section, it may be in the adult section under the same call number. Or vice versa.

If a book you want is not in the library right now, you can ask the librarian to reserve it for you or order it from another library. You may have to pay a small fee.

JUDGING A BOOK'S USEFULNESS

When you find a book that you think you can use, take it off the shelf and look at it. You need to figure out if it's worth checking out and taking home.

Check the table of contents and index. Can you tell if this book has information about your topic? Look in the table of contents. Then, for a more in-depth look, turn to the index. Look under your specific topic (*field mouse* in a book on rodents; *speeches* in a book on Abraham Lincoln). Then go to those pages and see if the information there is what you need.

There's also a nice trick, a shortcut, to see how much information about your topic is in the book. If you look in the index under, for example, *NFL draft picks*, and it says 45–47, then you know there are three straight pages in the book about NFL draft picks. If you look up *NFL draft picks* in another book's index and it says 45,

87, 92, you know that NFL draft picks are mentioned on three separate pages. Chances are, the book with three straight pages will give you more information. But you should check out the three separate pages just to make sure you're not missing something good.

Check the book for readability. Turn to a section you're interested in, and start to read it. If you can't understand what you're reading, you should find another book on the subject.

Check for a glossary. A glossary is very helpful if the subject has a lot of terms that are unfamiliar to you.

Check the copyright date. The more recent the book is, the more up-to-date the information.

READING THE BOOK

You may want to read the whole book, or you may just want to read the parts of the book that apply to your topic. Just as with an encyclopedia article, don't forget to read the captions, look at the pictures, and read any sidebars or boxes. Take good notes. As you're reading the book, continue to ask yourself, "What do I know? What do I need to know?" That will make you an efficient reader.

THE CATEGORIES OF THE DEWEY DECIMAL SYSTEM

There are ten main sections in the Dewey decimal system, and each section is broken down into smaller sections, which are broken down into even smaller sections.

000 is Generalities. (These are mainly reference books.) When you're ready to start your research project, go to the encyclopedias in the 030s.
100 is Philosophy and psychology. Do you want to find a book on ghosts? Try haunting the 130s.

40

200 is Religion. Want to read the story of the great flood? Bibles are shelved in the 220s.

300 is Social sciences. If you want to know what your teachers have read about education, try snooping in the 370s.

400 is Language. If you need a Spanish dictionary, *mire a los 460s.*

500 is Natural sciences and mathematics. Want to find books about animals? Hunt in the 590s.

600 is Technology (applied sciences). Do you dig farming? Plow through the 630s.

700 is the Arts. Dance on over to the 790s to read about—you guessed it!

800 is Literature and rhetoric. Would you like to read a Portuguese sonnet? Look in the 860s.

900 is Geography and history. Bounce on over to the 920s J to find a biography of Michael Jordan.

Note: Libraries do not use the Dewey decimal system to shelve fiction. Fiction is shelved alphabetically by author in a special fiction section of the library.

5

Magazines and Newspapers

If you need information that is current and up-to-date, magazines and newspapers are good places to look. An article in a magazine or newspaper can also give you details, pictures, and quotes you can use. It may lead you to experts you might want to interview later on.

You might also want to look in older magazines and newspapers. An older article, one that was written at the time something happened, will give you more details and more of a "you are there" feeling. For example, if you're doing a report on a person, you might get a lot of great details and quotes from the person in an article that was written five, ten, twenty, or thirty years ago.

If you were doing a report on Jim Henson, perhaps you could find a magazine interview with him. Then you could get direct quotations from the man himself. A magazine or newspaper article might also focus on one incident in a person's life in greater detail than a book would.

Your library should have a list of all the magazines

and newspapers they carry. You might be surprised how many magazines there are in the world, and in your library. Did you know there's a magazine (at least one) just about cats?

KINDS OF ARTICLES

Aside from general articles about a subject, keep in mind the many other kinds of articles that appear in magazines and newspapers:

Articles written by experts. Sometimes a person you are researching has written a magazine article herself. What better way to get inside that person's mind and work! Of course, the article might use technical terms and jargon. If that's the case, look for a popular summary of the article, or ask for help in "interpreting" it.

Articles in children's magazines. If you're researching a subject that is complicated, look for an article in a children's magazine. For example, if you are doing a report on a scientific subject, such as life in outer space, you might want to see if there's an article about it in *3-2-1 Contact* or *National Geographic World*, or in another kids' science magazine.

Obituaries. If you are doing a report on a famous person who is dead, see if you can find his or her obituary in a newspaper. *The New York Times* is a good one to try for national and international figures, and your town paper does obituaries of people who are well-known locally. An obituary is really a summary of a person's life. It will give you a lot of details and information.

A series of stories.

A newspaper is also good for following a story as it unfolds. You could look back and see how the Iran hostage crisis unfolded in 1979 and 1980, or you could research exploration of life on Mars through the Mars landing of 1997.

Headlines. It can be fun to put headlines in a report. Go back and find the headlines from when a man first walked on the moon, or when the Gulf War began and ended. You need to know the date or dates of the events to search in most old newspapers.

HOW TO FIND INFORMATION IN MAGAZINES AND NEWSPAPERS

To find information in magazines, use a magazine index. Many libraries have an index called *The Readers' Guide to Periodical Literature*. Look under the subject. *The Readers' Guide* tells you which magazines and newspapers have articles about that topic. The listings tell you the issue date of the periodical, the page numbers, and whether or not there are illustrations.

Many libraries also have their magazines on some kind of computerized index. (Wilson Disc and Infotrac are two companies that have magazine indexes on computer.) Again, search by subject. The listings will give you the same information that *The Readers' Guide* gives you. Ask your librarian for help the first time you use the system.

Most newspapers are not indexed. To look for information in a local or regional newspaper, you have to know the date of the event and search through old copies that way. However, some newspapers, such as *The New York Times*, are indexed so you can search by subject. The newer indexes are computerized, and some cover several newspapers. Tell your librarian what you're looking for, and ask her how you can find it.

The magazine and newspaper articles you find listed

in an index may be available in print form, or on CD-ROM, or you may have to read them on microfilm or microfiche, using special machines. Microfilm and microfiche are rolls and sheets of photographic film with pictures of magazine and newspaper pages on them. Because microfilm and microfiche allow many newspapers and magazines to be stored in a small space, libraries can have magazines and newspapers that go back decades. Ask the librarian for help locating the articles you want to read. You will also need help to use the microfilm or microfiche machines the first time.

You can access some magazines and newspapers on-line. The commercial on-line providers, such as America Online, have magazines and newspapers. And many more are available on the Internet. There is often a charge to use them.

READING THE ARTICLE

When you read an article in a magazine or newspaper, don't forget to read the sidebars and captions. Look at any pictures, graphs, charts, or diagrams. Can you use them in your report? Perhaps you want to make copies of them. Notice the way the author of the article has broken down the subject into different topics. Is that a good way for you to organize your report? Don't forget to take notes. And keep a list of the questions you still have to answer. There are still more places to look for information.

THE VERTICAL FILE

The vertical file is a filing cabinet in your library that is filled with newspaper clippings; magazine articles; pamphlets from the government and other organizations on a wide variety of subjects (safety, health, agriculture, food); photographs; maps; information about local events, people, and places; recipes; instructions on science fair and art projects; etc.

The newspaper clippings, papers, pamphlets, and so on, are put in folders that are arranged alphabetically by subject. At most libraries you can't take home the information you find in the vertical file, but you can read it in the library (and take notes) or make copies of what you need and take the copies home. As always, if you need help finding information in the vertical file, ask the reference librarian.

6

Visual Research

People often say that one picture is worth a thousand words. If a picture is worth a thousand words, can you imagine how many words a video is worth? A map? A painting? Think of visual research—photographs, paintings, videos, television programs, film strips—as another window into the subject you're investigating.

PHOTOGRAPHS, ILLUSTRATIONS, AND DIAGRAMS

When would it come in handy to see a picture of what you're writing about? Almost always! Pictures can answer questions, provide interesting details, and give you a different view of your subject, helping you to understand it in a way that words can't.

Look at the photographs you come across in your research, and write down your observations. You might be able to include those observations in your report. Sometimes you can include copies of the pictures themselves in your report. They can add a lot to your overall presentation.

Sometimes you can't find a photograph, or else the one you find isn't clear enough or detailed enough. In that case, you might want to look at an illustration or a diagram.

The camera has only been around since the 1800s. If you're researching something that happened before then, look for paintings and statues about your topic.

Finding Pictures

If you need a good photograph, illustration, or diagram, how do you find one? Start by keeping your eyes open as you go along. Many of the research sources you use will have pictures: magazines, books, newspapers, encyclopedias, CD-ROM encyclopedias, the Internet, museums, archives, information from tourist bureaus, pamphlets, and so on.

But what if you need an illustration of something and you haven't seen one? Then you're going to have to do some digging. For example, suppose you're doing a report on the archaeologist Mary Leakey. In your research, you have found out that when she was a little girl, she went on archaeological digs with her father and started collecting old stone tools, such as hand axes. It would add a lot to your report to include a drawing of a hand axe. But you need to find a picture of one to copy. How would you find it? Look up *stone tools* in the encyclopedia, or look in books about archaeology or paleo-anthropology.

You can also look for pictures in a visual dictionary, such as *What's What, The Dorling Kindersley Ultimate Visual Dictionary,* or *The Facts on File Visual Dictionary.*

Suppose you need a picture that is hard to find—for instance, some equipment used in mountain climbing. If you can't find a picture of it in books or magazines on mountain climbing, try the Internet. If you still come up empty, look in the index of the *Encyclopedia of Associations* under mountain climbing. Call or write to a mountain climbing group and ask for help. Always put your natural curiosity and nosiness to work whenever you're having difficulty finding something.

VIDEOS, MOVIES, AND TV

Believe it or not, another good way to do research is to watch videos and TV. Now you can't just sit down and watch your favorite sitcom to get reliable information. You have to watch shows about the subject you're researching. That usually means watching a documentary—a show that presents facts, interviews, and news clips about a historical, political, or social event, or a scientific subject.

If you're extremely lucky, a TV show about your topic will air just when you need it. Scan the TV schedule, looking for documentaries and biographies. There are regular TV shows, such as *Nature*, *Nova*, and *Biography*, that have documentaries on various subjects all the time. Some kids' shows, such as *The Magic School Bus* or *Bill Nye the Science Guy*, might have shows that could help you.

Keep in mind that you should evaluate the source before using any facts from the show. Use the same criteria you would use for evaluating any source.

If you have a VCR, tape the show as you're watching it so you can go back and look again at things that were particularly interesting.

Don't forget to take notes.

If you find out that a show on your topic has been on TV but isn't showing when you need it, you may be able to find it on video in your library or in the video store. If you can't find it, call the TV station that aired the show and ask to borrow or buy a video of the show. Be sure to tell them that you need it for a school report. They might be more willing to help you.

Finding the Right Video

Go to your local video store or your library, and look for a video on your subject. In the library, videos are usually indexed the same way books are—in the card or computer catalog. Type in the subject you're looking for (or the title if you know it). If the system allows, use the limiter VIDEO. For example, type in *Carson, Rachel* VIDEO or whatever is the correct format for the catalog you're using. (Ask the librarian.)

In the video store, ask the clerk. If the store has a computer that can look up videos by subject, or if the clerk knows the stock well, you're in luck. If not, browse through the documentary section.

If you can't find a video on your subject, your teacher or librarian may be able to help. They get catalogs from companies that rent and sell videos and films. Ask if you can look at a catalog, and see if there's a film or video that would be helpful. If it's going to cost money, make sure to check with your parents first.

You could also call an archive, special library, or organization to see if they have any videos on your topic. (See Chapter 10.) If they do, they might let you borrow one. If they don't want to let you walk off with it, ask if you might be able to view it on their VCR.

MAPS

If you're doing a report on a state, city or town, country, or region, look at a map of that area. Maps can give you great visual information. What rivers run through the town? Is it a place with a lot of highways? How far is it from the city to the ocean? Is the area mountainous or flat? Where is the state capital located?

Suppose you're doing a report on New Orleans, Louisiana. You pull out a map (maybe you look at an atlas in the library, or maybe you've sent away to

Louisiana for tourist information or gone to your local AAA so you can have your own map and look at it at home, or maybe you have a CD-ROM atlas for your computer). You see a lot right away. Water must be very important to the city of New Orleans. It is right on Lake Pontchartrain. It is near a lot of other water, too, such as Lake Borgne, the Mississippi Sound, and the Gulf of Mexico. You look at a close-up map of New Orleans, and you see that the Mississippi River runs right through downtown New Orleans. Looking at these maps, you can really get a feeling for New Orleans. You might want to include a map in your report so your readers can have that feeling, too.

7

The Internet

An exciting place to do research is the Internet. The Internet is a network of computers all over the world. Many computers in libraries, schools, and homes are set up to use the Internet. If you can't connect from home or school, ask your public librarian if you can do Internet research at the library.

Give yourself plenty of time to use the Internet. Plan in advance. First, you might have to make an appointment at school or at the public library to use it. Second, it may take you a while to find what you're looking for. Even experienced Internet users hit dead ends on-line. If you're new at it, you can expect to hit even more. But don't let this discourage you. There's a lot of information in cyberspace that would be useful for your report.

Check out Internet guides. This chapter will get you started doing research in cyberspace. But you should also take a look at Internet guides for kids. There are new ones coming out all the time. Ask your librarian or bookseller to recommend some good ones.

There are also Internet yellow pages and directories (for kids and adults) that can help you find Web sites, newsgroups, magazines, and other information on the Internet.

WEB SITES

A *Web site* is a group of pages on the World Wide Web, the part of the Internet that has pictures, sound, and video as well as text. A Web site may be put together by a person (an author, for example); a group (a fifth-grade class), an organization (the Chocolate Manufacturers Association); an institution (The New York Public Library); a museum (The British Museum), a government agency (NASA); or a state, city, or town.

When you are doing research on the Web, it is good to go to the Web site put together by an organization or institution, rather than by an individual. Those Web sites are usually more detailed, and the information is more likely to be accurate. Using the Internet can be a frustrating experience—an experience of going from lousy Web site to lousy Web site. But when you hit gold, it's terrific.

QUICK INTERNET DEFINITIONS

Browser: The software that helps you use the Internet. Two popular ones are Netscape Navigator and Microsoft Internet Explorer.

Commercial provider or Commercial on-line service: A way of hooking up to the Internet that has its own features, such as clubs, chat rooms, reference books, magazines and newspapers, and news. It costs money to belong to an on-line service. Two of the most-popular commercial providers are America Online and Prodigy.  There are also smaller, local Internet service providers that can hook you up to the Internet without all the extras.

Home page: The introductory page of a Web site. It tells you what is on the Web site. There are links on the home page that get you to other parts of the Web site and also to other Web sites.

Link: A piece of highlighted type that you click on to go from one part of a Web site to another part of the same site or from one Web site to another.

Lurk: To read newsgroup or mailing list messages, or a conversation going on in a chat room, without posting any messages or participating.

Search engine: Computer software available on the Internet that allows you to search for Web sites using key words. Some popular ones are Alta Vista, Yahoo!, and Lycos. Yahooligans! is a special search engine for kids.

URL: Universal Resource Locator—an address for a Web site. Usually begins with **http://**.

Web site: A group of pages on the World Wide Web created by a particular individual, group, or organization.

World Wide Web: The multimedia part of the Internet that has information in many forms, including print, pictures, sound, and video. The Web uses hypertext, a system that lets you jump from place to place using links.

A Web site can have only a few pages (even only one) or many. The New York Public Library's Web site has approximately 3,000 Web pages. The *home page* is the main page of the Web site. It's the page you get to first with the URL.

The *URL* is an Internet address. The URL **http:// www.nypl.org** is the address of The New York Public Library's home page, which will lead you to all of its 3,000 Web pages. Most URLs start with **http://**.

When you type a URL into your computer, you have to type it in exactly. That means the capitalization has to be exact and the slashes have to be in the right place. Make sure you're spelling everything correctly, too. (Some browsers have **http://** already there for you and you just have to type in the rest. But some require that you type in all of it.)

You can also get to another part of a Web site by typing in the specific URL for that page. For example, there are two ways to get to The New York Public Library's pages created for kids. You can either go to The New York Public Library's home page and click on the link to the Branch Libraries or you can type in the URL for "On-Lion" for kids, **http://www.nypl.org/ branch/kids/** or the URL for Teen Link, **http://www. nypl.org/branch/teen/**.

Links are those pieces of highlighted type that you click on to go from one part of a Web site to another part of the same site or from one Web site to another. Many Web pages have links to other related Web sites. If you are on a good Web site, following that site's links is a good way to get useful information. Your teacher or librarian may even have a Web site linked to other useful Web sites.

Here are a few Web sites that have been put together to help kids find information on the Web. They have links to many helpful sites:

🐾 *B.J. Pinchbeck's Homework Helper*
http://tristate.pgh.net/~pinch13/

🐾 *The Kids on the Web*
http://www.zen.org/~brendan/kids.html

🐾 *Kiddin' Around*
http://alexia.lis.uiuc.edu/~watts/kiddin.html

E-MAIL

E-mail is a way to send and receive letters to people all over the world in a matter of seconds. You need to have an e-mail account and address to send and receive e-mail. Some schools have e-mail addresses for students, and you might have e-mail at home. You also need to know the exact e-mail address of the person to whom you are writing, and you have to type it in exactly.

How can you use e-mail to do research? Think of it as a cheap phone call or a fast letter. Anything you'd do by phone or mail, you can do by e-mail. You can interview someone, ask for information from an expert or an organization, or send out a survey.

Be sure to follow the Internet's etiquette rules (see pages 73–74) when you send e-mail or participate in any Internet activity.

MAGAZINES AND NEWSPAPERS ON-LINE

Magazines and newspapers are great for finding current, topical information. Many magazines and newspapers have on-line editions, and there are also magazines that exist just on-line. Check your commercial service provider if you're hooked up to one. Most browsers and search engines have places you can click to look at what magazines are on-line. You can also use a search engine to type in the title of a magazine you'd like to look at.

Even magazines that are not on-line sometimes have a Web site. Most magazines have e-mail addresses, so you can write letters to the editor and request information. Look in your favorite magazine to see if it has a Web site or e-mail address.

SAFETY ON THE INTERNET

Because no one is in charge of the Internet, anybody can use it and put anything on it. Most of the people on-line are good, decent people and put out worthwhile information. But some people on-line are mean, obnoxious, and insulting. Some are even out to harm others. So just as you do in "real life," you need to follow some safety precautions in cyberspace.

Do not give out identifying information online. Don't give anyone your full name, address, phone number, or even your school name. (Chances are nobody's going to come hurt you, but why take any chances?) This applies to chat rooms, bulletin boards, newsgroups, and e-mail. Even if the Web site says you'll win a prize if you just fill in your name and address, don't do it.

Never agree to meet somebody you've met on-line without your parents being there. Someone could claim to be a ten-year-old girl but really be a forty-five-year-old man who has kidnapping on his mind. Even with your parents, arrange to meet in a public place, such as a mall or a restaurant.

Don't send your picture to someone you've "met" on-line without checking with your parents first.

Do not respond to an e-mail or a message that is obscene or threatening or suggestive or makes you feel uncomfortable in any way. Show the message to your parents, the librarian, or your teacher. Also forward a copy to your on-line service provider and ask for help.

If you come across a Web site that is obscene or threatening or makes you feel uncomfortable in any way, *leave it*. The same goes for bulletin boards, newsgroups, chat rooms, mailing lists, etc.

Report it. If you see something on the Internet that uses children in a bad way, or is damaging to children, tell your parents and report it to the

National Center for Missing and Exploited Children, either by calling 1-800-843-5678 or by contacting their Web site—**http://www.miss-ingkids.org**. Also report it to your on-line service.

Remember that not everything you read is true.

Don't stay on-line too long. It costs money, it hurts your eyes, and it can turn you into a zombie! Talk to your parents and decide with them what is a reasonable amount of time for you to be on-line.

Show your parents what you're doing on the Net. By showing them what you're finding, you will probably reassure them if they're concerned. And you will teach them, too. This is an area where you might know more than they do.

REFERENCE BOOKS

You can use reference books on-line just as you would use them in person. There are many reference books on-line—encyclopedias, dictionaries, books of quotations, thesauruses, and more. You'll find some reference books right at the New York Public Library Web site. You'll find many on commercial providers. For a list of the encyclopedias that are on-line, you can go to the search engine called Yahoo!

Here's how to do it. Type in this URL: **http://www.yahoo.com/Reference/Encyclopedia/**

You can do the same thing to get to dictionaries that are on-line. Just type in **Dictionaries** instead of **Encyclopedia** in the address above. You can also find a list of sites that have quotations by typing in **Quotations**. Try it for thesauruses, too.

NEWSGROUPS

Newsgroups are very large bulletin boards where people post messages. You can read the messages while you're on-line. You may also be able to save the messages to read off-line, depending on the setup you're using.

Newsgroups are set up by topics. You can get some valuable information by visiting newsgroups. Perhaps you are doing a report on rain-forest plants. You might want to go to a newsgroup where people are "talking" about the latest findings. However, you must remember that *anybody can say anything in a newsgroup*. You should not trust the information you find there. Think about it. You could post a message on a newsgroup saying you're a rain-forest biologist and you've discovered a plant (*Tropicalis orangejuiceious*) that gives eternal life. Somebody might believe you.

A good way to use newsgroups is to help you think of a topic. Or if you are interested in finding out people's opinions about a topic or in doing a survey, a newsgroup would be a great place to go.

How do you find newsgroups? You can use a search engine, but ask it to search newsgroups, not the Web. Using a search engine, you can go to *Dejanews*, which has all the newsgroups on the Internet listed.

FORUMS

Forums are the commercial on-line services' versions of newsgroups. Depending on which commercial provider they're on, they're called forums, special interest groups (or SIGS), bulletin boards, message boards, or clubs. The commercial providers often have very active forums. Search by your subject. Once you get there, you will probably see an icon to click on for message boards. When you get to the message boards, you'll find your subject broken up into many topics, with messages about each of those topics. Read through the messages for a while before you post anything. (This is called *lurk-ing.*) You might find information you need right there. By lurking you can also see the style of the forum and the kind of post you should leave.

All of the warnings about newsgroups also apply to fo-rums. Don't go to them for facts.

MAILING LISTS

Mailing lists are similar to newsgroups and forums. However, instead of conversations posted on message boards, these conversations take place through e-mail. You have to subscribe to a mailing list to be able to read the messages. If you're using a computer in a library, you won't be able to do that. But if you're using a com-puter at home, you can. Just be careful. If you join a mailing list, you could end up with hundreds of e-mail messages a day. It's probably not the best way to do re-search for a report. But it may be a good way to keep in touch with people who are interested in the same topic as you. Since most mailing lists are meant for adults, definitely talk it over with your parents before you sub-scribe to one.

CHAT ROOMS

Both the Internet and the commercial on-line services have chat rooms where you can go and talk to other people. They're not really rooms; they're places you navigate to on your computer. And you're not really talking, you're typing. But it is a live chat. You are typing to other people all over the world who are sitting in front of computers at the same time you are. Usually chat rooms have a subject: Japan, horses, writing fiction, video games, *Star Trek*, etc. Sometimes there is a guest in the chat room, or a specific topic. You can just lurk (read what others are saying), or you can ask a question or make a comment.

How can you do research in chat rooms? You can look for people who know a lot about a subject and ask them questions. You can also ask advice on how to get information from the Internet. Be warned, though, because people in chat rooms can say anything, which may or may not be accurate and may or may not be nice. David, a ten-year-old boy, went to a chat room whose topic was Japan. He wanted to find out what ten-year-old boys in Japan like to do in their spare time. He got some information (play video games and soccer), but he also saw some pretty nasty things—people cursing and making fun of other people.

To avoid an experience like David's, go to kids-only chat rooms. Or go to a forum about your topic and look for chats that are moderated by people who keep the participants in line.

SEARCH ENGINES

How do you find Web sites and newsgroups and other information on the Internet? If you know what you want and have its URL, you're home free. But what happens when you have a topic but don't know where to go to find out about it? Just as in the library you use magazine indexes and the catalog, on the Internet you use a search engine.

Some search engines are like book catalogs or indexes. Some are more like tables of contents. But all of them work in pretty much the same way. You can search by putting in a key word or phrase or by browsing through lists of subject areas. Some of the most popular search engines are Lycos, Alta Vista, Yahoo!, and Hotbot.

When you use a search engine, you type in a word or words. The search engine comes back with a list of "hits"—places on the Internet that contain the word or words you've typed in. There could be thousands upon thousands of "hits." That's why it's important to be as narrow and as specific you can with your search. If you type in a word that is too broad, you will get way too many "hits," and most of them will be misses. For example, if you're looking for information about marmosets, don't type in *monkeys*. You'll get too many sites that might not even have information about marmosets on them. Type in *marmosets*, and you'll get Web pages devoted just to your little monkey.

When you use a new search engine, read the help file first. This file will tell you how best to phrase your searches and queries. The file will also tell you how to limit or expand your search.

Remember Boolean operators? You can use them when you're searching the Web, too. Say you're looking for information on the history of chocolate. If you type in the word *chocolate*, you'll get all kinds of "hits," including many places that are just selling chocolate. But if you type in *chocolate* AND *history*, you'll get just what you're looking for—a site put out by the Chocolate Manufacturers Association and the National Confectioners Association. It has information about the history of chocolate, the growing of cocoa beans, and how chocolate is made. If you type in *chocolate* AND *factory*, you'll find a list of hits that include a tour of the Hershey chocolate factory. Unfortunately, as advanced as the Internet is getting, nobody has figured out how to get a chocolate bar from the computer screen into your mouth. Where *is* Willy Wonka when you need him?

Some search engines rate their "hits." You can ask a

search engine to give you just reviewed sites or just "green light" sites—those places the search engine's operators have decided are the best. Even better, some search engines, such as Lycos, have sites that they have decided are appropriate for kids. Try those sites first. You will probably get what you need there, and it will save you a lot of wasted time. It's frustrating to call up a site that either is written for physics professors or has inappropriate material on it.

Searching Tips

Refine your search. When your search engine comes back with a lot of misses instead of hits, or if it comes back with no hits at all, you should refine your search. Look at what you've typed in again. Were you as clear and as narrow as you could have been? Look back at your key word list for help.

Use more than one search engine. You might get more good hits with one search engine than with another. Experiment a little bit.

Choose the sites to look at. If the first few hits look good, that's a sign that you searched well. Now which sites should you go to? Scroll down and have a look at the whole page. Usually the search engine will limit the list to ten or twenty hits. Read the descriptions of the hits and decide on a few to check out. You'll probably want to check out some of the top hits first. You can always go back and look at more sites.

Don't waste time. Try to follow only those links that seem really good. You can fritter away hours looking at links that are dead ends, with your report deadline getting closer and closer. Again, to focus your research ask yourself, "What do I need to know?" Have a list of questions next to you while you're surfing the Net.

Check your spelling. Incorrect spelling results in misses instead of hits. So does typing in the wrong word or leaving out an important word of a phrase. As Mark Twain said (but not about Web sites!), "The difference between the *almost*-right word & the *right* word is really a large matter—it's the difference between the lightning bug and the lightning."

Browsing with Directory Search Engines
Choosing a topic. If you're looking for a topic to do a report on, look through an Internet directory, such as Yahoo! or Magellan. These subject indexes can be used like a table of contents. You can click up and down a list

of topics and see which ones grab you. It's a good way to browse and to narrow your search. Check out The New York Public Library Web site (**http://www.nypl. org**) for a list of these subject indexes.

Finding other key words. If you're having trouble finding information on a topic and need to look for other key words, try looking in an Internet directory.

Getting all different kinds of information. Some search engines also have links to other sites and databases, such as city maps, yellow and white pages of phone books, the day's news, and sports scores.

Finding kid-friendly things on the Web. Use Yahooligans!, which is especially for kids. Yahooligans! will link you to a lot of sites that you might find helpful. In your free time, explore it just for fun.

Remember David, the boy who was researching Japan? After his mixed experience with the chat room, David went to Yahooligans! and found a Web site that gave him a lot of information about Japan, including what kids do in their free time. Then he asked the authors of the Web site to help him find some Japanese kids to interview.

INTERNET ETIQUETTE

f you want to get reliable information, make friends, and have a good experience on the

Internet, you must have good Internet manners. These rules go for e-mail, chat rooms, forums, newsgroups, and mailing lists. Follow them, and you won't get "flamed"—which is the Internet equivalent of being insulted in a very loud voice.

Don't type in all capital letters or people will think you're SHOUTING at them.

Don't jump in on discussions in chat rooms,

newsgroups, or mailing lists right away. Hang back—or lurk—and see what people are talking about. Folks will get angry if you bring up a topic that was just discussed or if you introduce a new topic that doesn't fit.

Don't make jokes. When you make a joke in person, or even on the phone, people can tell you're kidding by the tone of your voice and the look on your face. In cyberspace they can't see or hear you. They might misunderstand and get insulted. One thing you can do is make it obvious that you're joking by putting a smile there :-), or a wink ;-) or <g>, which stands for grin. But when you first enter cyberspace, it's probably better not to make any jokes. *Definitely don't make jokes if you're interviewing an expert or writing a letter requesting information.*

Be polite. Use the same rules for politeness that you use in the "real" world. Say please and thank you, I'm sorry, and excuse me, if necessary.

8

Judging the Reliability of Sources

When you use a source in your research, you should do the best you can to make sure it is a source you can trust. You don't want to rely on information that is out of date, inaccurate, or biased. This applies to books, articles, Web sites, messages in newsgroups or on mailing lists, TV shows, videos, and even personal interviews. To evaluate the reliability of a source, you should ask yourself these questions:

How up-to-date is the information? This is especially important if you're researching a subject that is changing constantly, such as AIDS or computer technology. Check the copyright date of a book, the issue date of a magazine or newspaper article. Also check to see if a Web site has been updated recently. Most sites say somewhere when they were updated last. If a site hasn't been updated in a while, it doesn't necessarily mean it's a bad site, but it could be a sign that the author is not paying attention to the news about the topic.

If you already know a bit about the subject, see if the

author has included some recent information you know. If you are visiting a site or reading an article about the *Titanic*, for example, and you know there's new information about the ship that isn't there, that should tip

you off that the information is not up-to-date and may not be accurate. It may just mean the author hasn't had time to update the site, or that the magazine article was written before the most recent discovery, but it should set off some alarm bells for you.

Has the author cited sources? Is there a bibliography? Can you tell where the author has gotten his or her information? Is it from interviews with experts or from other books or articles? Or does it seem to be "off the cuff" and therefore not reliable?

Do you see any mistakes? After you've done a fair amount of research, you will know the subject pretty well. Look for any mistakes in facts or information. Also notice misspellings, typographical errors, and the like. These are indications that the book, article, or site has not been checked over very well and may have inaccurate information.

Is it well written? A good test of a source is how well it is written. If it is grammatically incorrect or sloppy, find other sources.

Is the source well balanced? Is it fact or opinion? If you're researching a controversial subject, you want to look at your source to see if it presents both sides of the issue. If the article, book, or Web site is the opinion of one person, *it should state so clearly*. If the author says something is his or her opinion, you can take that into account. If the author does not admit that what he or she is writing is opinion and not fact, it is not a reliable source. You will be able to tell if you read carefully that the author is showing only one side of an argument.

Also beware of crazy, off-the-wall statements, such as, "The government is hiding the fact that aliens from Titan and Ganymede are running the United States." Sometimes it is obvious that a Web site is just giving opinions. You can often tell because it sounds like the person is shouting.

For a Web site: Is there an e-mail address to which you can write with your questions? If you have any questions about the information on the Web site, you should be able to e-mail the authors and ask your questions. Do they provide an e-mail address or a place to ask questions?

How complete is the source? For a book, ask yourself, does it have a useful index? A bibliography? Does your source—book, article, video, Web site—cover the subject well?

Use at least three sources. You should not rely on one Web site, book, or article for your information. Do not use only the Internet as a source of information. If three books say that the *Titanic* sank because it hit an iceberg and one Web site says it sank because aliens from Mars abducted it and then bored holes in its side, guess which piece of information you should throw out? Usually it won't be so obvious, of course. But the rule of thumb is to find three sources that say the same thing. If you can't find three consistent sources when you write up your report, indicate that your sources disagree. It will show that you did a lot of research and that you are a good, critical researcher.

9

Sending Away for Information

You can get books, pamphlets, maps, illustrations, photographs, and other print materials by sending away for them. Many historic sites, museums, government agencies, businesses, organizations and associations are willing to send information to students. They may even have information prepared especially for kids doing research.

Your librarian might be able to suggest the best places to send for information about your topic. He or she also can show you books on how to get free materials. And some of the sources you are already using might mention places you can send away to.

In order to be able to use the information you receive, you must *keep in mind your time frame*. The time it takes to get information by mail varies a lot—from as short as one week to as long as a month or six weeks. Be sure to ask when you call how long it will take to get the information you are requesting. If it seems as though you won't get the information in time, ask if they can rush it. If they can't, ask if they know of another place that could send you the same kind of information more quickly.

TOURIST BUREAUS AND CHAMBERS OF COMMERCE

If you're doing research about a state—your own or another—you should call the state's tourist bureau. You can find the 800 numbers (toll free) for all fifty states in the *World Almanac*. (You can also find them on-line. Search on your commercial service or through a search engine under the name of the state.)

When you call the 800 number, tell the person who answers the phone that you're doing a report on the state and would like information. He or she will either connect you to the right person or will take down your name and address.

Some states have material specifically for students doing reports. These are usually sheets with facts, figures, and statistics. (For example, North Carolina's fact sheet tells you that the state dog is the Plott hound. If you look in a dog encyclopedia for a picture and more information about the Plott hound and put that in your report on North Carolina, your teacher will be impressed by your dogged research.)

States will also send you:

🐾 colorful brochures and pamphlets of the state's tourist sites and historical attractions,

🐾 maps,

🐾 pamphlets of facts and history,

🐾 pamphlets of cultural information,

🐾 visitors' and travel guides that tell you everything

from highway rules to what sites to see to where to stay,

🐾 brochures of individual attractions,

🐾 calendars of events (which will give you insight
into the state's customs, pastimes, and industries).

The great thing about the materials you receive by
mail is that they are yours to keep. So you can cut out
pictures or maps to use in your report.

If you're doing a report on a particular city, town, or
county, you should call the local chamber of commerce.
From them you will get information about tourist attractions, climate information, and population statistics. To
get the phone number of your local chamber of commerce, look in the telephone book under *Chamber of
Commerce*. To find out the number for the chamber of
commerce in a different area, look in the *World Chamber
of Commerce Directory*. If your library does not have
that, you can look in the phone book for that area. If
your library does not have either, you can call
Information for that area and ask for it. To call
Information, find out the area code (available in the
front of any phone book) and dial 1 plus the area code
plus 555-1212. (For example, the Information number
for Hawaii is 1-808-555-1212.) There is a charge to call
Information, so ask your parents before you call. You
can also look on the Internet by searching under the
town's or county's name.

ORGANIZATIONS AND ASSOCIATIONS

There are organizations and associations devoted to certain topics. For example, there are organizations for different hobbies, sports, and breeds of dogs. You can ask these organizations to send you information. You can also ask them questions or ask them to recommend experts to interview. For example, if you are doing research on a certain breed of dog, contact that breed's association. You can ask for any magazines or newspapers they publish, pamphlets, fact sheets, pictures, and maybe even a video.

How do you find these organizations?

After you check your sources to see if they mention any associations, societies, or organizations, you should check the following resources for more ideas.

Almanacs have listings of associations, societies, and organizations. Another place to look is a book called *Chase's Calendar of Events*. It's a listing of all the special days that are sponsored by people and special groups. If you look in the index under your topic, you might find just the group or expert you need.

A great place to check is in a reference set called the *Encyclopedia of Associations*. In the *Encyclopedia of Associations* you can look in the index under the subject you're interested in, and you'll find listings for associations devoted to that subject. Each listing gives you the address, phone number, and contact person, as well as information about the group and whether they have publications.

You'd be surprised what there are associations for. Here's a small sampling: Antique Airplane Association; Automobile License Plate Collectors Association; National Carousel Association; American Cat Fanciers Association; Clowns of America, International; Conchologists of America; International Club for Collectors of Hatpins and Hatpin Holders; International Association of Calculator Collectors; an association for every breed of dog; clubs for games such as checkers, dominoes, and backgammon; about six chess associations; the Goldfish Society of America; and the Burlington Liars Club—as well as, of course, many more serious ones, such as Citizens for a Drug-Free America; National Student Campaign Against Hunger and Homelessness; and the National Council of Teachers of English.

When you ask for information, tell the person why you want it. "I am in sixth grade, and I am doing a report on golden retrievers." He or she should be happy to help you.

OTHER PLACES TO SEND AWAY FOR INFORMATION

Banks, not for money, but for pamphlets about money, information about mortgages, interest rates, currency exchange, foreign money

Companies, for information about their products, the history of the company or the industry, recipes, photographs

Government agencies, for information on just about anything. Some examples: food safety guidelines, energy efficiency, educational guidelines, list of endangered species

Historical sites, for pamphlets with information and pictures

Movie companies, for information on how movies are made, history of movies, posters, photographs, as well as information on particular movies, actors

Museums, for brochures of exhibits, information about painters and paintings, information about the museum itself

Publishers, for book catalogs, posters, bookmarks, reading campaigns

Sports teams, for information on the team, the players, and the game, posters, photographs

Zoos, for brochures and pamphlets on exhibits, particular animals, schedules, habitats

10

Research Trips

You might not find everything you need for your research project in your library, on the Internet, or in materials you send away for. How else can you get information? You can go on trips! You can do research in other libraries—special kinds of libraries. You can also take a trip to a historical site, a museum, a zoo, or even to your local grocery store.

OTHER LIBRARIES

Your library doesn't have everything you need? Try another one. Sometimes regular public libraries have special collections, such as collections on the history of radio and TV broadcasting, cooking, farming in your area, or weaving. Some libraries have collections of very old and rare books, or first-edition children's books.

There are also special libraries devoted to one or a few subjects. All the books, pamphlets, magazines, and primary sources are on that subject. There are libraries devoted to birds, cars, hobbies, the Civil War, the

Revolutionary War, American Indians, and many other topics.

Genealogical libraries have oral histories (stories that people told about themselves and their families that somebody wrote down), census materials, and vital statistics (here you could find out how many people lived in your area in the 1890s, for example).

Your local library should have a listing of special libraries and libraries with special collections in your area. Look through the listing to see if any would be helpful.

Also call organizations, associations, agencies, and institutions. Many of them have libraries. If you are having trouble finding information, see if you can visit the headquarters of a group or the library of an institution that specializes in your topic or your topic area. For example, one fifth grader was having trouble finding information on Elizabeth Blackwell. She went to the local hospital and used the library to find information on the first woman to become a doctor.

Once you've found a library that you'd like to visit, call ahead to ask for the hours of the library and whether or not you can take out books. Very often these special libraries will not allow you to take books home. Ask if the library has a photocopier. If so, make sure to bring change. Also, *don't forget to bring your note-taking materials.*

HISTORICAL SOCIETIES

Historical societies are organizations that are devoted to history, often a certain period in history. A historical society has collections of books, photographs, letters, and documents, as well as exhibits on local history, a specific event or time period (such as the Revolutionary War or colonial days or Civil War battles), or a specific topic. One historical library has a collection of books about the history of the circus in America.

You might want to take pictures of some of the artifacts or materials in the exhibit, but be sure to ask permission first. Flash photography can damage old documents and materials.

Consider talking to the curator (the person who put together the exhibit) or the guides at the historical society. The people who work there know a lot about the subject.

MUSEUMS

There are many topics that you can research at a museum—topics in science, technology, history, art, and culture. Ask at your library for a listing of museums in your area. Look for natural history museums, art museums, science museums, and museums devoted to particular topics, such as trains, tools, or Chinese culture and history.

If you are doing a report on dinosaurs, go to a natural history museum and look at some real dinosaur bones. If you're doing research on pioneer days, go to a museum that has pioneer wagons and cooking equipment on display. There are museum villages where people act out the life of a certain time period and area. Are you researching Vincent van Gogh? Is there a museum nearby that has a van Gogh painting?

While you're at the museum, collect brochures, and take pictures if they're allowed. (Always ask before you take pictures; some museums do not allow photography.) If you can't take pictures, you might want to sketch some of the exhibits. Ask questions of museum workers or interview the curator.

Many museums also have libraries that focus on the theme of the museum. Find out if you can look at the materials in the library. For example, at a railway museum, you might be able to look at railroad maps, pictures showing the construction of railroads, and correspondence files about the building and running of a railroad. Use the library as you would any library. Take notes and make photocopies if you can.

Check out the gift shop for books if you still need some information. You could also buy copies of artifacts, postcards with reproductions of paintings on them, brochures, stickers—things that would jazz up your report.

HISTORICAL SITES

If you are researching a historical person, event, time period, or place, a visit to the related historical site (or sites) is invaluable. There is nothing like firsthand observation, even a hundred or two hundred years later. Historical sites often are refurbished to look just as they looked when a famous person lived there or when the building or site was important in history. Visit a battlefield, a government building, a historical figure's house, a one-room schoolhouse, a plantation, a gold mine, etc.

Find out new facts. (Thomas Jefferson's gravestone doesn't say that he was president of the United States.)

Find answers to questions you have. (Are there any animals on Ellis Island?)

Collect free information to use in your report. (A diagram of a Civil War battle.)

Buy some inexpensive souvenirs to use in your report or presentation. (A postcard with a portrait of Henry Ford.)

Observe and collect details. After visiting a battlefield, you might write: "The hill the Confederates had to climb was so steep, a twelve-year-old boy who is a star soccer player had to stop three times before he made it to the top."

From a visit to a historical figure's home: "On a cold winter afternoon, the sun streamed into the governor's mansion, warming up the desk where he made the decision to . . ."

Take a lot of notes while you are there, with as many details as possible (such as the sun streaming in through the window). Make sure to write down the date you visited. You'll need it for your bibliography.

Check your facts. If you write down that somebody's bedroom was painted blue, check with the guide to make certain that the bedroom was blue when that person lived there. Similarly, if there is a hedge of bushes at a battle site, check to make sure those bushes were there when the battle took place (although you could still write: "Where a hedge of shrubs now stands, fifty men died.").

If you can't get to a historical site, call or write and ask the guides to send you pamphlets, pictures, and other information. You could also interview a guide or a curator—just be sure to have specific questions ready ("What color was Thomas Jefferson's office in Monticello?" "What kind of plants were there on Bunker Hill?"). Another thing you could do is interview somebody who has been there and get his or her firsthand observations.

ZOOS

Are you doing a report on a marmoset? A penguin? A Siberian tiger? Go to a zoo and get a close-up look at the animal you are researching. Before you go to the zoo, call first to find out:

🐾 if the zoo has the animal you're interested in,

🐾 what time the animal is fed and if you can observe the feeding, and

🐾 when the animal is most likely to be awake.

Here are some tips for your visit:

Take notes. What color is the animal? How big is it? What does it eat? How much does it eat? Is it awake or asleep? Does that jibe with your knowledge of it being nocturnal or diurnal? What is its zoo habitat? Has the zoo replicated its natural habitat? Does the animal seem interested in you? Is it interested in the other animals in its cage?

Ask a guide or zookeeper any questions you still have. Tell him or her that you are doing a report for school. You might be able to get a closer look at an animal (a nondangerous one) than a regular zoo visitor.

Bring a camera. Take a few pictures in case one doesn't turn out. Ask a parent or friend to take a picture of you in front of the animal's cage.

Check out the library. If the zoo has a library, allow some extra time to see if it has any information you could use in your research.

Visit the zoo gift shop to see if there's anything there you can include in your report, such as full-color post-cards of your animal, stickers, or printed material you can use in your research.

RELIGIOUS RESEARCH

If you're doing research about a religious topic, go right to the experts. Many churches and synagogues, Buddhist temples, mosques, Quaker meeting houses, etc., have information about their religion that they'd happily give out to you. Look in your phone book in the yellow pages under *Churches*. Churches are listed by denomination. There will be a heading that says, for example, *Churches—Baptist* and then a list of Baptist churches with their addresses and phone numbers.

When you call, explain why you are calling, being as specific as you can. For example, you might say, "I'm doing a report for school on the way different people get married. Could you please send me a copy of your marriage ceremony?"

If your research is more general, ask if there is a library you could use where you could find out more about the religion. Be sure to ask for the hours of the library and whether or not you can take out books.

When you visit the religious institution, be respectful of the customs there. Put on a hat or take off your shoes if necessary. Always ask if it is okay to take photographs or make sketches.

COMPANIES, BUSINESSES, FACTORIES

Depending on your topic, you might find it useful to visit a company, such as a stock brokerage; a business, such as a sign painter; or a factory, such as an automobile maker, in your area. You might want to interview somebody there, watch the operation of the factory, observe how the business works, or look at materials in the library.

Call first to make an appointment. Tell the person who answers why you are calling. You will probably need to speak to someone in the public relations, customer relations, or communications department. Ask if you should bring an adult with you.

ARCHIVES—INCLUDING YOUR OWN ATTIC

Try to get some primary sources in your research. Primary sources are items such as letters, papers, official documents, statistical records, photographs, manuscripts, interviews, and objects.

A good place to find primary sources is in an archive, where they have been collected and preserved for the historical record. Most countries have national archives, where you would find the first drafts, for example, of important speeches or proclamations. Institutions such as companies and universities have archives as well. There are archives devoted to famous people. If you were researching a person, it would be great to visit the archive where his or her papers are stored. There you might find photographs, video and cassette tapes of interviews, and even personal memorabilia.

Ask the reference librarian in your public library if he or she knows of an archive that would have primary sources on your topic.

An official archive is not the only place you will find primary sources. You can find some great archival material closer to home—such as in your basement or closet, or in your great-aunt Agnes's attic, your next-door neighbor's cousin's garage, an antique store, or the laboratory of a scientist at the local college. You will have to do some detective work to find out where you can, for example, read some letters home from soldiers, or look at some photographs from the sixties, or try typing on an old manual typewriter.

Be sure you get permission to quote any letters or reproduce any pictures, of course. And you should credit the person who owns the primary source in the bibliography at the end of your report.

Remember that letters and other primary sources are great for details but may not be great for objective reporting or facts. For example, if you are doing a report on a war and read a soldier's letter home, you should use details such as what he ate for dinner, and how he felt, and which of his buddies was killed. But you should double-check any major facts about the war that he might relate, such as how many people had been killed so far or how far from the border a certain town was.

EVERYDAY PLACES
You don't have to go too far afield to do some first-rate firsthand research. What you're looking for might be in a place you go to all the time.

GREAT PRIMARY SOURCES

Here are some examples of primary sources you could use:

🐾 The weather bureau's statistics of the amount of rainfall over the past one hundred years

🐾 The birth certificate or marriage certificate of a person you're researching

🐾 Photographs of immigrants to the U.S. in the early 1900s

🐾 A mortar and pestle used to grind spices

🐾 Test tubes, Bunsen burners, and the microscope used by a scientist you're researching

🐾 Diary entries

🐾 Personal letters

🐾 The manuscript of a famous book

🐾 Your great-grandmother's handwritten recipes

🐾 Your great-grandfather's expense ledger from college

For example, if you're doing a report on beef production in the United States, go to the supermarket and talk to the meat manager. Make an appointment first. Call up and ask to talk to the person in charge of meat. Tell him or her that you are doing a report on beef in the United States and would like to see what beef looks like when it comes to the supermarket. You probably will get a tour behind the scenes at the supermarket and will be able to walk into the huge refrigerator where the beef is stored and watch a butcher cut up a side of a cow into steaks. (This could make you a vegetarian.)

You could also visit a supermarket for a report on grains, dairy foods, marketing, product placement (why do they put some things at the end of the aisle?), advertising, or which ethnic groups are in your area and what foods they eat.

Before you do your research, make sure you figure out what it is you need to find out. Write down some questions in a notebook. Bring the notebook and a pencil or pen to write down the answers to your questions and to record your observations. You might end up asking somebody a few questions. If you do, make sure you write down his or her name and title to include in your bibliography.

PLACES TO DO RESEARCH YOU MIGHT NOT THINK OF

Here are some other everyday, and not so everyday, places you might be able to use for your research. Remember, research can be creative and fun. See what else you can add to this list.

- The post office
- A pharmacy
- A department store
- A restaurant (the kitchen in a restaurant, too)
- A plant nursery or florist
- A toy store
- A computer store

- Your doctor's office
- A pretzel factory
- The police station
- The ambulance squad
- A hospital
- The room where 911 calls come in
- An accounting firm
- A jewelry store
- An art gallery
- A video arcade
- A hardware store
- A gym

11

Interviewing People

Very often a person is the best source after you've done some background research. The person you are going to interview might be an expert in the field—a historian, scientist, or writer. Or he or she could be a "regular" person who knows a lot about your subject (your uncle Jeff, who is a Civil War buff, or your next-door neighbor, who travels to China all the time). Or he or she could have lived through something you're researching (your grandmother, who can tell you what life was like during the Depression, or your math teacher, who fought in Vietnam). The person could be someone you know or don't know. The important thing is to interview someone who has something to offer you about your subject.

HOW TO FIND PEOPLE TO INTERVIEW

The grapevine. One way to find someone to interview is through people you know. Tell your family, friends, parents of friends, neighbors, etc., that you are looking for somebody to interview about a certain subject.

Your sources. Did the reporter who wrote the newspaper article about the chance of life on Mars interview somebody? Probably. Would that somebody talk to you? Maybe. If you want to interview an expert or a famous person, you have to be prepared to be turned down. But you might get lucky.

First you have to find the expert. If you know the organization or university or institution the expert works for, you just have to call that place and ask for the person you want to interview. To get the number of the place he or she works, you can look it up in the phone book, call Information in that city or look in a reference book. Ask your librarian for help.

The yellow pages. Look in the yellow pages of your phone book for experts in many fields. For example, if you're doing a report on plants in your area, look under *Landscapers* or *Nurseries* for someone to interview.

The *Encyclopedia of Associations*. This encyclopedia is a great resource for experts. Look in the index for your topic and find the associations that will help you find experts on that subject.

The Internet. You can use the Internet to find people to interview. For example, you can find children in other countries who could answer your questions about daily life in their country. One way to find kids in other countries is to go to Web sites about those countries. Another is through an on-line pen pal organization such as *kidlink*, which you can get to from Lycos and other search engines.

You can use the Internet to find experts on-line, too. Using a kid-oriented search engine like Yahooligans! or from a Web site for kids (such as The New York Public Library teen page [**http://www.nypl.org/branch/teen/ homework.html**]) you can find experts on many topics. There are also specific Web sites set up to answer your questions about various subjects.

You can also use forums or clubs to find people to interview. If you were doing a report on a children's book author, you could go to an on-line club for children's book authors and post a message that says, "I am doing a report on Greata Writer. If any of you know her personally and would be willing to be interviewed by e-mail, I would appreciate it." You might be lucky enough to get an answer from one of her friends—or from the author herself.

You can also find specific people by searching in Yahoo!'s people search. Perhaps a person was mentioned or quoted in a magazine article you read, but you don't know where to find him or her. You have to know the person's first and last name. It is also helpful to know where he or she lives.

SETTING UP THE INTERVIEW

So you've decided whom you want to interview. Now you have to set up the time and place. Make sure you call the person well before your deadline in case he or she is busy and can't talk to you for a week.

Now, how do you convince the person you want to interview that he or she should let you? If it's your grandmother, or your father, or your best friend's mother, it's probably not going to be too hard. But you still have to act like a professional and treat the person and your project with respect.

If it's someone you know well, a phone call will do. Let's say you're doing a report on Mexico, and your aunt visits Mexico often for work. When you call her up, you should say something like this:

"Aunt Ginny, I am doing a report on Mexico for my social studies class. If it wouldn't be too much trouble, I would like to interview you about Mexico. Could we set up a time to do that?" You can also add how long you think it will take. "I think this will take about thirty minutes." Or "I have about ten questions."

Before you call her, know what questions you want to ask, just in case she says, "This would be a perfect time." You don't want to have to say that you're not ready. Also, some people might ask you for the questions in advance or for an idea of the kinds of questions you'll be asking. Chances are, though, that she will say something like, "Why don't you call me back (or come over) tomorrow?"

If the person you want to interview is not someone you know, or not someone you know well (for example, the man who runs the corner grocery store, or a zookeeper), it would be best to write a letter and follow that up with a phone call. Make sure you have the correct spelling of the person's name, the person's title, and the person's address. Here is a sample interview request letter:

```
Mr. Glen Headly
Owner
Headly's Grocery Store
159 Main Street
Verity, North Carolina 54321


Dear Mr. Headly:
   I am a fifth grader at Doyle Elementary
School. My family shops at your store all
the time.
```

I am doing a report on apple growing in America. Since most apples are grown in the North and Northwest, I would be very interested in talking to you about your part in bringing apples to people here in the South.

Would it be possible for me to interview you on the subject? I don't think I would take more than half an hour of your time.

My deadline is in three weeks. I hope it is all right with you if I call early next week to set up a time for us to talk. If you would like to reach me before that, my phone number is 555-6363.

Sincerely,
Amanda Pruett

When you call, ask when would be the best time to interview him. If you need your mother's or father's help getting to the store, have ready a list of times when they can drive you, so you're not running back and forth between the person you're going to interview and your parents trying to set up a time.

If you don't know the person well, do the interview in a public place or bring a parent with you. In any case, make sure your parent knows where you will be.

If your interviewee would like to conduct the interview over the phone, and there is no particular reason why you can't, then respect his or her wishes.

THE QUESTIONS

Always, always, always make up your questions before you do the interview. Think clearly about what you need to know. Remember to ask yourself, "What do I know? What do I need to know?" Make your questions specific, not general.

For example, if you're interviewing your great-aunt's best friend's next-door neighbor about what it was like in Ireland when she was growing up there, don't ask, "What was it like while you were growing up?" Ask much more specific questions: "Where did you live in Ireland—in a town, a city, or in the country?" and "Did you have any pets?" Also, make sure your questions are in a good order and follow from one another. For example, if you want to find out about her school life, put all the questions about school together. "Did you go to school?" "For how many years?" "How many children were in your school?" "What subjects did you have?" "Who was your favorite teacher?"

Even though you will make up the questions ahead of time, always be prepared to ask a new question you hadn't thought of if your interviewee says something interesting. This is called a follow-up question. For example, if she says, "My favorite teacher was Mrs. Crawford because she brought in the strangest snacks for us to eat." Don't ask, "What was your favorite subject?" even if that was the next question on your list. Instead ask, "What were some of the strange snacks she brought in?"

If your interviewee goes off the subject, but it's great stuff, let her go. You may not have known before your interview that you wanted to know about a legend that said a family of leprechauns baked cookies for the entire town every Saturday, but it will add a lot to your report.

But if she goes off the subject and it's not helpful or you're not interested, gently bring her back by asking the next question.

Beware of yes-or-no answers. Try to word your questions so that the person can't just answer yes or no. (Or at least have a follow-up question ready if she does.) A simple example: Instead of asking, "Did you have any brothers or sisters?" ask, "How many brothers and sisters did you have?"

HOW TO CONDUCT THE INTERVIEW

Whether you conduct your interview in person or on the phone, you'll have a choice to make. Do you tape the interview on a tape recorder, or do you take notes? There are advantages to each.

Using a Tape Recorder

Taping the interview can be the easiest way to keep a record of your conversation. If the tape recorder works, you will have every word that your interviewee said. You won't have to worry about getting her words down exactly, which can be a frantic activity. After the interview, you can play back the tape and slowly write down exactly what he or she said. However, not everyone feels comfortable being taped. Make sure to ask permission to tape the interview.

There are two big drawbacks to using a tape recorder. One is that if the tape recorder breaks, you have lost everything. The other problem is that if your interview goes on for a long time, you will have a lot to transcribe. But there are ways around these problems.

Before you do the interview, make sure to test your tape recorder. Make sure it is working by interviewing your mom or dad or baby brother. If you're going to do the interview over the phone, call your best friend and interview him. You need a special attachment to tape over the phone. You can't just put a tape recorder nearby. Some answering machines can be used to record an interview.

Make sure you have new batteries or plug in the recorder. Bring an extra tape with you in case the one you are using breaks or you need an extra one. Remember to turn over the tape when the first side is used up. Before you do the interview, check to see how much time you have on the tape. A ninety-minute tape has forty-five minutes on each side. Check your watch when you start the interview and keep an eye on it so you turn over the tape in time and don't lose anything.

Just to be sure you get your answers, take notes, too, even when you tape an interview.

Taking Notes by Hand
Many professional writers say it is a lot easier in the long run not to use a tape recorder but to write down

the answers. You can take your notes longhand or on a computer.

When you make up your list of questions, write the questions in such a way that you can write the answers right underneath. Remember to leave plenty of room for follow-up questions. Some people write only one question per page.

Make sure you have enough paper and more than one writing utensil. It can be pretty embarrassing to have to stop an interview because your pencil point broke, your pen ran out of ink, or you have to go find some more paper.

Don't be afraid to ask your interviewee to slow down if you are having trouble keeping up. Make sure you write neatly enough so that you will be able to read your handwriting! Use abbreviations to help your writing go faster.

Thank-You Note

When you end the interview, thank your interviewee very much for her time. Politely ask if you can call her if you have any more questions. Get her address if you don't already have it. The minute you get home or get off the phone, write a thank-you note. It can be very simple.

May 15, 1998

Dear Mrs. Crawford,

   Thank you so much for letting me interview you for my report on Ireland. I know
your memories and insights will add so
much to my paper. I had a good time talking with you. I hope to see you again
sometime.

   Thank you again.

   Sincerely,
   Wanda Fulchild

Put the note in the mail immediately. Your interviewee
will think, "What a wonderful, polite child!" and will also
be more willing to answer some more questions and
help you fact check later.

CONDUCTING AN INTERVIEW BY MAIL

Sometimes it will not be possible for you to conduct the
interview either by phone or in person. Perhaps the
person is in a different country. Perhaps your parents
do not want you to make a long-distance phone call.

Perhaps the person is too shy to meet you in person or has trouble hearing over the telephone. You can still do the interview. You will just have to do it by mail, by e-mail, or in an on-line chat room. If you're doing the interview on-line in "real time," conduct the interview just as you would in person or on the phone. Just make sure you save a copy onto your computer memory before you sign off-line.

If you're doing the interview by mail or e-mail, the procedure is a little different. First of all, because you will not be able to ask follow-up questions right away, ask at the outset if you'll be able to send more questions along after the first interview. You can explain why. "You might say something really interesting that makes me think of a question I hadn't asked. Could I write back and ask you some follow-up questions?"

When you write your questions, make sure they are clear, understandable, written neatly (if handwritten), and spelled correctly. You might want to show your questions to a parent or teacher before you send them out. *Make sure you send out your questions in plenty of time.* Ask your interviewee to have the answers back to you by a certain date. Give him or her at least a week. When setting that date, leave plenty of time for follow-up questions.

INTERVIEW FOLLOW-UP

After you've done your interview, read it over. Is there anything that is unclear or confusing? Are there any facts you need to check? Contact the person you interviewed to answer any more questions you have or to check facts. Make sure you have accurate quotes and facts before you include the interview in your research.

As a courtesy, send a copy of your finished report, including the interview, to the person you interviewed. If you have time, give her a copy before you hand it in, just in case she catches any mistakes or thinks of something she wants to add.

12

Surveys

Suppose you want to conduct the same interview with a lot of people. That is called a survey. A survey is a good way to get the same information from a large number of people. Perhaps you're doing a report on music in America. You decide it would be interesting to know how many kids in your school take music lessons, and what kind. You could find out by conducting a survey. Perhaps you are writing a report on the recent election in your town. You could conduct a survey to find out how many people voted, whom they voted for, and what were the issues that were important to them.

Before you write up your survey, you need to figure out the following things:

What do you hope to find out? This will determine the questions you write.

Whom are you going to give the survey to? (Children, adults, both? People you know, people you don't know?) If you're surveying children, you might write the survey differently than if you're surveying adults. If you're surveying people you know or who know you, the survey will be different than if you're surveying people who don't know you.

How many people do you want to take your survey? This will determine how it is conducted (in person, by mail, etc.).

Is anybody going to help you conduct the survey? Do you need help getting the survey to as many people as possible?

WRITING THE SURVEY

Make sure you get the basic statistical information about the people you are surveying. In other words, who are they? Have questions they can fill out to find out their gender, age, grade, etc.

You want to write the survey so that it will be easy for you to tabulate the answers. The best way to do that is to write questions that have choices. You don't want to have open-ended questions; they are almost impossible to tabulate. A common format is three or four choices plus "other."

Suppose you are doing research on chocolate. For part of your report you want to find out how popular chocolate is among kids, and how they like to consume their chocolate. So you write up a survey. You want to make your questions specific so they're easy to tabulate, but not too specific so that someone filling it out might have trouble picking the right answer. You wouldn't ask only, Do you like Mounds or Nestlé Crunch? What if someone doesn't like either? Take a look at this sample survey. Warning: It might make you hungry.

The Chocolate Survey

1. What is your favorite way to have chocolate?
   a) chocolate candy
   b) chocolate cake or brownies
   c) chocolate pudding
   d) chocolate ice cream (including shakes)
   e) chocolate milk
   f) other (for example, "chocolate-covered
      ants")_____

2. How often do you have chocolate?
   a) every day
   b) three to six times a week
   c) once or twice a week

d) oncc a month

e) once a year or less

Now if you want to get more specific about something, you can break down one of the categories.

3. When you eat chocolate candy bars, do you prefer

a) plain chocolate, with nothing mixed in

b) chocolate with nuts

c) chocolate that crunches

d) chocolate with peanut butter

e) chocolate with caramel

f) other (for example, candy-covered chocolate)_____

4. How often do your parents let you have chocolate?

a) whenever I want

b) never, I have to sneak it

c) only if I really beg

d) once a week

e) once a year

5. You are a

a) girl

b) boy

6. How old are you?

a) 5 or under

b) 6–8

c) 9–11

d) 12–14

e) 15–18

f) other_____

CONDUCTING THE SURVEY

If you are going to survey a fairly small number of people, you'll probably want to do it in person. Perhaps you
can get some friends or family to help you ask your survey questions.

Three girls were doing a report on smoking habits in the United States. One of the parts of their report was a survey. They planned to do their survey at school, in their neighborhoods, in local malls, and downtown. They started in their public library. One of the girls went over to a woman and very shyly asked if she could ask her some questions. By the time she approached the twentieth person, she was not so shy. But she was always polite and respectful.

Going person-to-person is a great way to do a survey, especially if you have more than one person conducting the survey, time to do a widespread sample, and transportation to get to various places. But if any of those conditions is a problem, or if you want to have a larger sampling, you will probably have to make copies of your survey and mail them or deliver copies to houses or classrooms with a note saying when you will be back to collect them. Not everybody will fill out the survey, so you should probably deliver them to more people than you need.

Another way to conduct a survey is over the computer. You might want to e-mail your survey to people you know. Or, if you need a wider sampling, you could post your survey to a mailing list, on message boards, or to a newsgroup.

Try it out first. Do the survey with a small sample of people before you pass it out to the larger group. After you get back the first answers, you'll have a chance to revise the survey if you need to. Have you missed any questions? Is it going to be easy to tabulate the results? Are there questions you should take away or add? Rewrite the survey if necessary before you pass it around some more.

TABULATING AND PRESENTING THE RESULTS

Once you have conducted the survey, you will need to tabulate the results so you can present the information. Since you have set up the survey neatly, you should be able to add up the answers fairly easily. Have a friend read out the answers to you as you tally the results.

Your results may look something like this:

Question #1. What is your favorite way to have chocolate?
   a) chocolate candy—100
   b) chocolate cake or brownies—20
   c) chocolate pudding—3
   d) chocolate ice cream (including shakes)—62

e) chocolate milk—18
f) other (for example,"chocolate-covered ants")—
   30—mostly joke answers, a few interesting
   ones such as chocolate-covered coffee beans;
   straight chocolate syrup; chocolate chip cookies—10 people said that (that should have
   been an answer!)

You might write up the results like this:

> Most people in our survey like to eat their
> chocolate in candy form. But a lot of people like
> to eat chocolate ice cream. The next most popular
> ways to eat chocolate are chocolate cake or
> brownies, chocolate milk, and chocolate chip
> cookies. One person likes to eat chocolate syrup
> straight from the bottle; another loves chocolate-
> covered coffee beans.

You could also write up the information as statistics.
For example, you could sum up the answers to question 3 like this:

> When the people surveyed eat chocolate candy

bars, the overwhelming majority (63%) like chocolate with caramel. A mere 2% likes chocolate with nuts. The rest are fairly evenly divided. Ten percent like chocolate with peanut butter; 12% like chocolate that crunches; 9% like plain chocolate. The rest, 4%, chose other, with most of the write-in choices being candy-covered chocolate and chocolate-covered mints.

When you present the results, make sure to include how many people you surveyed (300) and who they were (150 boys and 150 girls, all between the ages of nine and fourteen). You can break down the results further by tabulating which kind of candy ten-year-old boys like vs. ten-year-old girls, for example.

13

Hands-on Research

Sometimes doing research means doing it yourself. Hands-on research includes observing the world around you, performing experiments, making things, trying out activities or doing manual labor, and even cooking.

OBSERVATIONS

Whenever possible, firsthand observations should be part of your research.

For which topics could you include your own firsthand observations? There must be hundreds, but here are just a few to get you started thinking: Worms, bees, slugs, ants, pigeons, birds' nests, how leaves change color, cats, dogs, goldfish, roots, the water cycle, weather, rocks, the subway system, bridges, elevators, pulleys, cranes, and tractors. Whenever you're researching a

topic, ask yourself if you can go see it for yourself. It might be as close as your own backyard.

EXPERIMENTS

Even if your teacher didn't tell you to, you could include an experiment in your research. Be creative, but be realistic. Choose an experiment you can do and that would add to your report. Your experiment should answer questions that you have about your topic. ("What do I need to know?") Plant a lima bean and watch it grow. How tall does it get? Plant two or more for comparison. Does it do better in shade or in sun? Inside or outside? Get some caterpillars and see if they'll turn into butterflies or moths. Find out if your braces are magnetic.

COOKING AND EATING

Perhaps you are doing a report about early American pioneers, or Japanese immigrants, or slaves in the South. It would add a lot to your report to include a section about what they ate.

If you can't find out what they ate in the more regular sources, such as encyclopedias and books, you can hunt on the Internet, ask people you know, or ask a librarian. He or she might be able to help you find a cookbook that is from that time or from that group of people. (As far as pioneer foods go, for example, there's *The Little*

House Cookbook: Frontier Foods from Laura Ingalls Wilder's Classic Stories by Barbara M. Walker.)

The next step is to taste the food and describe it yourself. You will have to convince your mom or dad to either take you to the right restaurant, or to help you make the food. Pick out a simple recipe, such as cornbread, and volunteer to not only help make it but also to clean up all the dishes.

MAKING AND DOING THINGS YOURSELF

Perhaps you're researching something that you can try for yourself. For example, if you're researching an artist, see if you can copy one of his works of art, maybe even using the same materials he used. If you're researching early humans, try to make your own tool out of a stone. If you're researching Native Americans, make a god's eye or a medicine pouch.

You can also try to do things the way that people used to do them, or the way they do them in another country now. Wash clothes on a washboard, use a mortar and pestle to grind corn, or read by candlelight.

When you do hands-on research, you really put yourself into the world you are researching. It will make the subject more meaningful for you and will add a lot to your finished report.

A SAMPLE EXPERIMENT

Question: Will a leaf change color if it is not on a tree?

🐾 State your hypothesis: No, it won't, because it needs to get chemical signals from the tree to change color.

🐾 Perform your experiment: Pull a green leaf off a tree.

🐾 Observe.

🐾 Record observations. (You can do this in writing and also by taking photographs or making drawings.)

🐾 Compare. Are the leaves still on the trees turning color?

🐾 Draw your conclusion.

🐾 Write up your experiment, and include it in your report.

PAT YOURSELF ON THE BACK

You're done! You have a pile of 3″ x 5″ cards, a folder of photos, the tape of an interview, and a pan of cornbread. The answer to "What do I know?" is "A whole lot!" and the answer to "What do I need to know?" is "Nothing." You *may* still find a few small holes to fill in while you're writing, but you are done with the bulk of your research, and you should feel great. You're an expert on your subject. And the next time you have to do research, it will be that much easier because you will use the same skills you developed this time. Congratulations!

Now it's time to write up your report. It's going to be easier than you think, because you did your research so well.

But first, pat yourself on the back for the great research job you've done.

INDEX

A
almanac(s), 23, 80, 83
archive(s), 97–98
associations, 49, 79, 83–84, 104
atlas(es), 23, 52

B
bibliography
    in sources, 76, 78
    information needed for, 26, 92,
        98, 100
book(s)
    about books for children, 24
    judging usefulness of, 37–38
    on specific topics, 21, 29–40
    reading for research, 38
Boolean operators, 33–34, 69

C
call numbers, 35–37
captions, 19, 38, 45
catalog, book, 30–35
    how to look up a book, 30–31
    how to search by subject, 32–35
    using limiters on, 33
chambers of commerce, 80–82
cooking, 127–128
copyright date, 16, 26, 38, 75

D
Dewey decimal system, 35–37
    categories of, 39–40
dictionary(ies), 11–13, 24
    biographical, 23
    on line, 64
    visual, 49
documentary(ies), 49–50

E
e-mail, 59–60, 78
encyclopedia, using, 13–22

article, reading, 19–21
CD-ROM, 15, 18
heads and subheads in, 19–21
looking up a topic in, 17–18
on line, 64
special encyclopedias, 21–22
Encyclopedia of Associations, 49,
    83–84, 104
experiments, 127, 129
expert(s),15, 41, 42, 60, 76, 83,
    95, 103, 104–106, 130

F
facts, checking, 92–93, 98, 114,
    116
field guide(s), 23

G
government agencies, 79, 85
historical sites
    getting information from, 79,
        85, 93
    visiting, 91–93

H
historical societies, 89

I
index, 16–18, 37–38, 49, 78, 83
    for newspapers and magazines,
        44–45
information
    sending away for, 79–86
    telephone number, 82
Internet, 54–74
    books of quotations on, 64
    browser(s), 56
    bulletin boards, 65–66
    chat rooms, 66–67, 73
    definitions of terms, 56–57
    dictionaries on, 64

O

organizations, 79, 83–84

P

pictures, 12, 19, 38, 45, 47–49, 95
  how to find, 48–49
places, everyday, 98, 99–102
plagiarism, 26
primary sources, 97–99
pronunciation, 12

Q

quotation books, 24
  on-line, 64

R

reference books, 11-28
  kinds of, 22–24
  on-line, 63–64
reference section, 11, 22–24
reliability of sources, 75–78
religious institutions, 95–96
research
  definition of, viii, 26
  hands-on, 126–129
  sources for, viii, 9, 25, 48, 75–78, 79
  trips, 87–102

S

search, electronic
  in book catalog, 32–35
  on CD ROM encyclopedia, 18
  on Internet, 68–72
  using limiters, 33, 51
  using Boolean operators, 33–34, 69
sources, *see also* research, sources for
  judging reliability of, 75–78
  primary, 97–99

souvenirs, using, 91, 92, 95
states (U.S.), materials from, 80–82
subject, *see also* topic
  searching by, 18, 32–35, 44
surveys, 117–125
  conducting, 121–123
  sample survey, 119–121
  tabulating results, 123–125
  writing, 118–121

T

tape recorder, 111–112
telephone book(s), 24, 72, 82, 95, 104
telephone information, 82
television shows, 49–50
thesaurus(es), 24, 34
  on-line, 64
topic, *see also* subject
  books on specific topics, 29–40
  choosing a, 1–4, 71–72
  looking up in encyclopedia, 17–18
tourist bureaus, 80–82
trips to do research, 87–102

V

vertical file, 46
videotapes, 49–52
visual research, 47–53

WXYZ

Web site(s), 55, 57, 58–59, 64, 72, 78, 105
  searching for, 68-72
World Wide Web, 55, 57
zoo(s), 86, 93–95

ACKNOWLEDGMENTS

Thank you to the following librarians, who were generous with their insights into what kids need to know to do good research: Jonathan R. Betz-Zall, Sno-Isle Regional Library System, Edmonds, WA; Rebecca Brown, Takoma Park Library, Takoma, MD; Nancy Bujold, Rochester Hills Public Library, Rochester Hills, MN; James B. Casey, Oak Lawn Library, Oak Lawn, IL; Carolyn Caywood, Virginia Beach Public Library, Virginia Beach, VA; Jan Dickler, Bucks County Free Library, Doylestown, PA; Larry Dunsker, Bucks County Free Library, Doylestown, PA; Lois Fundis, Mary H. Weir Public Library, Weirton, WV; Deborah Glessner, Hillcrest Elementary School, Holland, PA; Teresa Hanas, Bucks County Free Library, Doylestown, PA; Torrie Hodgson, Burlington Public Library, Burlington, WA; Bill Hollands, Seattle, WA; Nancy Jackisch, Oshkosh Public Library, Oshkosh, WI; Marijo Kist, Acacia Branch Library, Phoenix, AZ; Gloria Liposchak, Johnson County Library, Overland Park, KS; Donna Miller, Craig-Moffat County Library, Craig, CO; Lorie O'Donnell, Jervis Public Library, Rome, NY; Janet Russell, Clayton Community Library, Concord, CA; Loann Scarpato, Abington Friends School, Jenkintown, PA; Karen Seaton, Buckingham Friends School, Lahaska, PA; Irene Sever, Haifa University, Haifa, Israel; Sandra Strandtmann, Juneau Public Libraries, Juneau, AK; Shawna Saavedra Thorup; Teri Titus, Belmont Branch Library, Belmont, CA; Lorrie Wheeler, Tuscarawas County Public Library, New Philadelphia, OH; Melissa Yates, Buckingham Elementary School, Buckingham, PA; Rhonda Yates, Zion-Benton Public Library District, Zion, IL; Denise Zielinski, Helen M. Plum Memorial Library, Lombard, IL; Cathy Zilber, Eldredge Public Library, Chatham, MA. And special thanks to Jeff Cramer, Boston Public Library, Boston, MA, for finding so many of these librarians.

In addition to the librarians who served on the New York Public Library advisory board for this book, three others read and critiqued all or part of the manuscript: David Rosensweig, New York Public Library Information Technology Group, and Shaaron Warne and Roberta Yancovich, Bucks County Free Library, Doylestown, PA. I'm grateful to them for providing me further perspective and much helpful advice.